MY BODY POWER!

**Body Confidence Guide:
For Girls
Tweens, Teens & Young Adults
Ultimate Body Positivity Toolkit!**

Conquer the Fear of Puberty, Body Perception, & Find Love for Your Growing Body

Part of the **MY POWER!** Series
Book 3

♥♥

SheriBelle Karper

Kingman Publications LLC

Copyright ©2025 by SheriBelle Karper

All rights reserved. Worldwide rights reserved.

No portion of this book may be reproduced in any form without written permission from the publisher or the author, except as permitted by U.S. copyright law. No part of this book may be reproduced, distributed, or transmitted in any form or by any means, including photocopying, recording, or other electronic or mechanical methods, without the prior written permission of the publisher or the author, except in the case of brief quotations embodied in critical reviews and certain other non-commercial uses permitted by copyright law.

This is a work of nonfiction. This publication is designed to provide accurate and authoritative information in regard to the subject matter covered. However, it is sold with the understanding that the author and the publisher are not engaged in rendering medical, legal, investment, accounting, doctoral, or other professional services. While the publisher and author have used their best efforts in preparing this book, they make no representations or warranties with respect to the accuracy or completeness of the contents of this book and specifically disclaim any implied warranties of merchantability or fitness for a particular purpose. The material provided is for informational, educational, and entertainment purposes only and should not be considered a substitute for professional advice or consultation from qualified authorities in the relevant fields. Readers should consult professionals or experts in specific areas for advice suited to their individual needs. No warranty may be created or extended by sales representatives or written sales materials. The advice and strategies contained herein may not be suitable for your situation. You should consult with a professional when appropriate. Neither the publisher nor the author assumes any responsibility or liability for any errors, omissions, or potential consequences from the application of the information provided within this book, nor shall they be liable for any loss of profit or any other commercial or personal damages, including but not limited to special, incidental, consequential, personal, or other damages.

Disclaimer: Names, characters, and incidents are either the product of the author's imagination or used fictitiously. Any resemblance to actual persons, either living or dead, events, or locales is purely coincidental.

ISBN: 978-1-967750-00-9 (paperback) • LCCN: 2025910282 (paperback)

ISBN: 978-1-967750-01-6 (ebook)

ISBN: 978-1-967750-15-3 (hardback)

ISBN: 978-1-967750-18-4 (audiobook)

Printed in the United States of America

1st Edition ©2025

Ultimate Puberty Guide to Empowerment and Body Positivity

MY BODY POWER!

Body Confidence Guide

For Girls
Tweens, Teens and Young Adults

By SheriBelle Karper

FOR GIRLS

Conquer the Fear of Puberty and Body Perception

KP KINGMAN PUBLICATIONS

Contents

MY BODY POWER!	1
Foreword By Dr. Renee Cotter, MD, OB/GYN, FACOG	7
Dedications	9
Epigraph	11
1. Hey There, Fabulous Reader!	13
2. Puberty Unpacked—The Ultimate Upgrade!	21
3. What's Happening and When?	25
4. But, I Don't Want to Grow Up	29
5. Curves Are Cool!	35
6. What's Happening to My Face?	43
7. Growth Spurts!	51
8. Hair? Down There?	55
9. Welcome to the Period Club!	59
10. Make a Difference with Your Review	69
11. Shape and Weight Changes During Puberty	71
12. What's That Smell?... Body Odor and Care of Your Body	75
13. Eating Well and Feeling Great!	87
14. Sleep: The Importance of Those Zzz's!	95
15. Growing Up: We're Also Talking About Emotions	99
16. Exercise: Move Your Way to Happy!	109
17. Let's Compare… Let's Not!	115
18. Support Crew: Creating Your Own Circle of Awesome	123
19. Role Models: Finding Your Squad of Superstars!	129
20. Fashion and Expression	139
21. Embracing Your Unique Sparkle	143
22. Kindness is Your Superpower!	149
23. Most Important Chapter in this Book, and I'm Not Kidding!	155
Acknowledgements	161
About the Author	163
Other Titles by SheriBelle Karper	167
Glossary and Words to Know	171
Resources & References	179

Foreword By Dr. Renee Cotter, MD, OB/GYN, FACOG

As an obstetrician and gynecologist with over 30 years of experience in Southern California, I have dedicated my career to supporting women through the various stages of their lives. From the early years of puberty to the complexities of menopause, I have witnessed the profound physical and emotional changes that define womanhood. It is from this perspective that I wholeheartedly endorse SheriBelle Karper's invaluable guides *MY PERIOD POWER!*, *MY SOCIAL POWER!* and *MY BODY POWER!*

These books offer not just information, but a compassionate roadmap through the often daunting journey of puberty. SheriBelle masterfully navigates the physical transformations and the emotional landscapes that accompany this pivotal time, providing practical advice and heartfelt encouragement to help young adults embrace their evolving identities.

In *MY SOCIAL POWER!*, SheriBelle goes beyond the basics of physical care; she addresses the emotional and social challenges that can arise during this tumultuous period. Her insights into navigating social media and making safe choices are particularly relevant in today's digital age, where young teens face pressures that many of us from earlier generations can hardly imagine. By using language that resonates with young readers, SheriBelle ensures that her messages are not only accessible but also engaging.

Reflecting on my own experiences, I realize how fortunate I am to have grown up in a time without the influence of social media. After reading *MY BODY POWER!*, I realize again that conversations about menstruation or sexuality were often hushed, leaving many of us to navigate these changes in silence. *MY PERIOD POWER!* reminds me of the awkward moment of telling my mother I had started my period, only to receive a brief response about where to find pads. This lack of open dialogue fueled my passion for women's health and highlighted the necessity for clear, supportive resources.

MY PERIOD POWER!, MY SOCIAL POWER! and *MY BODY POWER!* are essential tools for young adults and should be seen as vital references for parents, educators, and healthcare professionals alike. They empower young readers to not only understand their bodies but to celebrate them. I envision a future where every young teen receives a copy of these books as a rite of passage, guiding them through the challenges of puberty with confidence and grace.

I encourage everyone who cares for or mentors young teens to embrace SheriBelle's work. Together, we can foster a generation of informed, empowered young adults who love themselves and their bodies.

Dr. Renee Cotter, MD, OB/GYN, FACOG

Dedications

To My Parents…
Thank you for the gift of curiosity.

♥

To my pre-period self…
Don't worry about it. It's all going to be fine.

♥

To my family…
I know I drove you crazy, so thank you for sticking with me.

Epigraph

A girl should be two things: who and what she wants.
— Coco Chanel

♥

Be yourself; everyone else is already taken.
— Oscar Wilde

♥

I believe in being strong when everything seems to be going wrong. I believe that happy girls are the prettiest girls. I believe that tomorrow is another day, and I believe in miracles.
— Audrey Hepburn

♥

The trick is growing up without growing old.
— Casey Stengel

1. Hey There, Fabulous Reader!

Let me ask you something: Have you ever been lying in bed, staring at the ceiling, replaying a moment from school where you said the wrong thing and thought, "Why am I like this?!" Or maybe you've been scrolling through social media, wondering why everyone else looks like they're living a movie while you're just trying not to trip over your own feet in the hallway?

You are NOT alone. Growing up? It's like a never-ending game of dodgeball—you're just trying to make it through without getting smacked in the face. Your body is changing, friendships are shifting, emotions are all over the place, and social media is constantly screaming at you about how you are supposed to look, act, and be. It's A LOT.

And that's exactly why I wrote ***MY BODY POWER!***

Not Your Average Book!

This book is your all-in-one guide, your confidence coach in book form, here to help you handle all the wild changes in your body and your social world like a total boss. Think of it as your coolest, most supportive BFF—the one who hypes you up, tells you the truth, and reminds you that you're already amazing just as you are.

It's written like how people talk, no boring textbook vibes here. We're keeping it real, fun, and full of smiles (because let's be honest, smiling makes everything better).

But don't let the jokes fool you. This book is full of important stuff. We're diving deep into body changes, self-love, social pressures, friendships, and everything in between.

What We'll Talk About:

- **How Your Body is Changing:** Yep, from breast buds to deodorant (Yikes!) and periods (Double Yikes!). It's all happening, and we're going to make sense of it together.
- **Comparisons:** How not to fall into the trap of comparing yourself to every airbrushed celebrity and influencer out there.
- **Taking Care of Your Body:** Grooming, exercise, and the art of giving your body some tender loving care.
- **Body Timeline:** With all these changes, find out what to expect and when.
- **Self-Expression & Confidence:** From fashion to personality, we'll talk about how to own your vibe and shine in your own unique way.
- **Mental Health & Body Image:** Because how you feel about yourself matters just as much as how you see yourself.

- **Support Systems & Role Models:** The people you surround yourself with matter. We'll talk about how to find the best squad to lift you up.
- **Growth Spurts:** You might suddenly shoot up in height (Whaaat?), which can feel pretty weird, happen pretty fast, and sometimes feel a bit awkward. This is the most obvious sign that puberty has begun.
- **Body Shape Changes:** Boys' chests get broader and more muscular. Girls get curvier, their hips wider, and breasts start to grow. (Eeeeek!) We get to go bra shopping! *Cha-ching!* It's like your body is sculpting itself into its new adult form.
- **Voice Changes:** Boys' voices crack and deepen. Sometimes it's a little funny, but try not to laugh because guys are really self-conscious about it. Girls' voices might change a little also, but it's less dramatic.
- **Hair, Hair, Everywhere!** Yes, hair starts growing in new places: Underarms, legs, and around your private parts. Boys might even grow facial hair.
- **Skin Wars: Hello, Acne!** Hormones can make your skin oilier, leading to pimples on your face, and even on your back. Annoying, but still totally typical for puberty. (UGH. I know.)
- **Emotional Changes—The Inner Journey:** Puberty isn't just about your body, your brain is also changing. It can make you think and feel differently. You might start looking at the world more like adults do and asking big questions. This is a time to discover more about who you are, what you believe in, and who you want to become.
- **Mood Rollercoaster:** Feeling happy one minute and sad the next? Yep, those are your hormones working overtime. It's like your emotions are getting a workout, too.

By the end of this book, you'll have everything you need to own your power, love your body, and crush this whole growing up thing.

Are You Ready to Unlock Your Power?

This book is about helping you step into your boldest, most confident self. Because confidence isn't about being perfect, it's about showing up for yourself, embracing who you are, and knowing that you are already enough. Hey, if you love this book, be sure to check out my other guides.

Introducing: The multi-book MY POWER! Series of Confidence and Success!

Meet Your Other BFFs: The Companion Books!

<u>**MY PERIOD POWER!**</u> (For Girl Tweens, Teens and Young Adults). It's a <u>PERIOD</u> CONFIDENCE GUIDE, where you'll learn everything you want and need to know about your period, dealing with guys, mood swings, and stuff like that. We'll learn how to handle all these changes together and have a lot of fun along the way. You can get it at the same place you got this book. Super cool, eh?

Plus, you'll want to buy <u>**MY SOCIAL POWER!**</u> (For Boy & Girl Tweens, Teens and Young Adults) It's your go-to <u>SOCIAL</u> CONFIDENCE GUIDE, full of tips and tricks to help you figure out your super unique and always evolving thoughts and group interactions. It's about learning how to handle social situations like a pro, feeling good about yourself, and owning your vibe no matter what's happening

Hey There, Fabulous Reader!

around you in this wild, fast-moving world. Let's crush it together!

Soon, the **_MY PERIOD POWER! WORKBOOK_** (For Girl Tweens, Teens and Young Adults) where you can journal, predict your period schedule, and monitor your moods, along with fun puzzles, recipes, and beautiful coloring pages. You can find it in the same place you got this book. Fun!

And, also the **_MY SOCIAL POWER! WORKBOOK_** (For Boy & Girl Tweens, Teens and Young Adults) which will contain journaling, goal-setting, gratitude listing, prompts for writing, and other great things! This will also be available where you found this book.

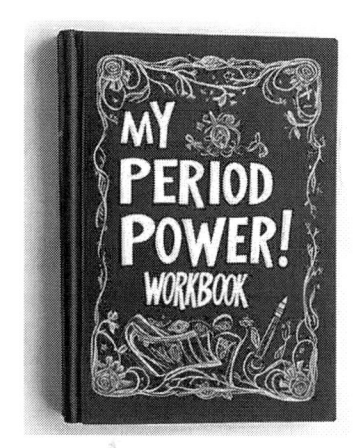

This book contains the word "girl" and other feminine terms because I think that's who will probably read it. But hey, if that word doesn't fit with who you are, swap it out for a word that fits you better. That way, you will still get all the awesome info in this book.

So, Who Am I?

Let me introduce myself! I'm SheriBelle Karper, and I guess you could say that confidence is kind of my thing.

Please make sure you take a look at the **About the Author** section in the back of the book (seriously, go ahead and read it later). You'll see I've done some pretty epic stuff in my life, stuff you can totally do too. Why? Because it all comes down to choices and figuring out what's important to you.

Anything is possible… or impossible… it all depends on how you look at life. I personally like the word possible much more than impossible… "Possible" gets you places. "Impossible" keeps you stuck.

Make sure you check out the amazing **Foreword written by Dr. Renee Cotter, OB/GYN!** I just feel so honored that she wanted to be a part of this book, and she made her endorsement plainly clear in her phenomenal foreword. She's a very popular gynecologist and obstetrician for over 30 years in Los Angeles, California. So please, go ahead and check it out!

Confidence isn't about knowing everything or being perfect, it's about showing up for yourself, trying new things even if they feel scary, and embracing your fabulous, one-of-a-kind self.

Mistakes? Pfffft. That's how we grow.

So this book? It's all about helping you unlock the power you already have inside you. Yep, it's been there all along, like a treasure chest, just waiting for you to crack it open. You were actually born with everything you need.

Yes, everything is possible.

By the time you read the last page in this book, you'll be a total pro about your body and about how your body fits into this world. You'll know the ins and outs, the ups and downs, and all the science behind the magic. It's like you'll become a body expert, and you'll be able to share what you've learned with your friends. This book will give you the courage to handle anything that comes your way. Pretty exciting, huh?

It's Important To Ask Questions and Have Conversations

Got a question? Or are you super curious about something? That's great! Talk about it with your parents or a trusted adult. They can even get their own copy of this book and you both read along at the same time. You'll have some great and inspiring conversations, and it will be low-key, AMAZING! (Seriously!) Or, maybe talk with a teacher or your doctor. Just make sure it's someone that BOTH you AND your family trust.

We'll get into all these topics and help you navigate them like a pro. You are awesome just as you are, and this book will help you boost your body confidence even more. Imagine feeling totally in tune with all the changes going on inside you and owning it. That's the goal!

Going through puberty, dealing with social issues, and mastering your body changes are like unlocking a superpower. Sure, it might feel like a lot at first, but once you own it, you'll feel unstoppable. Think about it… knowing all this about your body puts you in control.

I Know It's a Lot of Information, But There's an Old Saying…

"How do you eat an elephant? You eat it one bite at a time." — Francis of Assisi and Desmond Tutu

Now, we are not literally going to go out and eat elephants! Hahaha, NO! What it means is that we have this huge project that is impossible to handle all at once…

1. We're going to break it down and take each word, each idea, each bite, one nibble at a time…
2. We're going to consume each idea one by one by learning them and applying each of them to ourselves…

3. And then, we're going to use these ideas to grow into an even more amazing person!

Ready to eat that elephant? Let's do this! Game on!
ACTION TAKEAWAYS:

- This is not your average book. It's written like how people talk to each other.
- Puberty takes a long time to complete, so be patient with yourself. It can start anywhere from ages 8 to 16, and it's different for everyone.
- You are growing into something amazing! Change is good, but sometimes change is not always easy. It might feel weird to be changing, but it's all part of growing into the superstar you are meant to be. Embrace it!
- Get ***MY SOCIAL POWER!*** (For Boy & Girl Tweens, Teens and Young Adults),
- And ***MY PERIOD POWER!*** (For Girl Tweens, Teens and Young Adults), and
- Plus, ***MY SOCIAL POWER! WORKBOOK*** (For Boy & Girl Tweens, Teens and Young Adults)
- Along with ***MY PERIOD POWER! WORKBOOK*** (For Girl Tweens, Teens and Young Adults), to help you through these big changes in your life. Ask questions. Get answers. Be a good listener and make sure you hear the answers correctly and then work that great advice into your life.

2. Puberty Unpacked—The Ultimate Upgrade!

Welcome to your teen years! This is when your body starts a project, like a major room makeover. It's called **PUBERTY.**

Puberty? What's That?

Puberty is like hitting the big, shiny red upgrade button for your body and mind. It's the stage where you shift from the kid version to the adult version of YOU, and it can be as wild as any video game you've ever played.

Growing Up: The Body Remix

Have you felt like you went to bed one size and woke up another? Totally weird, but also totally normal. Your body is doing exactly what it's meant to do—grow up! This chapter is all about getting to know your changing body, figuring out what's happening, and totally rocking those changes. All this change doesn't happen only to girls; a different type of puberty happens to boys, too.

Puberty is not a race, and it doesn't start and finish overnight. It's a gradual process that usually starts between the ages of 8 and 14, but could begin at 16 and still be normal. It gets your body ready to have babies someday (way down the road). Since having babies is probably not on your to-do list right now, it's important to know this is a reality.

During puberty, your body will begin developing in new ways. You'll start your menstrual cycle (called "getting your period"). You will take care of yourself more than ever—your health, your choices, your whole vibe! And, it will be a lifelong job. You will start looking out for you!

The Brain Boss Starts Calling the Shots

It all begins in your brain. Yup, that impressive grey matter that is squished between your ears. *Yeah, that stuff.* The puberty magic begins in a tiny place called the hypothalamus. It's like the control center that sends out signals to get taller and grow hair in weird places.

It then tells another part of your brain, the pituitary gland, to send out hormones. These hormones press the start button and puberty gets rolling. It's like it's saying, "Hey, wake up! It's time to grow up!" These hormones kick start a bunch of changes in your body.

Hormones: The Body's Messengers

Hormones are like messengers zipping around your body, telling it to turn things up a notch. For girls, it's stuff like your breasts getting bigger and getting your period (yep, we'll get into that in a moment).

The Cool Side of Puberty

Now here's the cool part: Puberty is packed with awesome upgrades, even though sometimes it feels awkward and challenging. You'll get stronger, smarter, and more capable of making decisions. You'll learn about becoming more independent, which is a huge part of becoming an adult.

Navigating the Changes

You might be thinking, "Whoa, I didn't ask for any of this!" It's totally okay to feel unsure about all these changes. Talking it out helps a lot. Chat with your parents, your friends who are also going through the same things, and other adults you trust. Remember, everyone has been through this or is going through it, and they can be awesome allies.

So yeah, puberty is a major life update with all sorts of new features to explore. It gets you ready for the amazing adult things you can do in the future. Think of it as leveling up in the game of life. You'll unlock new skills, face new challenges, and discover cool new parts of yourself. It might sound like a lot, but it's all part of growing up. Keep in mind that everyone goes through it, and it's nothing you can't handle.

Ready... Set... Grow!

ACTION TAKEAWAYS:

- Your body will go through a lot of changes.
- Puberty is your body's upgrade! Puberty is like hitting the big, shiny upgrade button for your body and mind. It's your own personal remix into the adult version of you.
- It all starts in the brain. It sends out hormones to tell your body that it's time to grow and change.

- Hormones are your body's messengers that trigger everything from body changes to mood swings. Yes, they can be a bit wild, but they help you grow up.
- Puberty can feel awkward, but it's packed with some awesome upgrades like more independence, getting stronger, and figuring out who you are.
- Got questions? Talk it out with your parents or a trusted adult.

3. What's Happening and When?

Puberty is like your body's personal amusement park ride—lots of ups, downs, and sudden changes. Are you wondering what will happen and when? Let's break down the typical timeline so you can get a sneak peek at the ride. Everyone's journey is a little different, so these ages are just rough guidelines.

Ages 8 to 10: Early Signs

For some, puberty kicks off around ages 8 to 10. You might not see much on the outside, but your body is already starting the engine.

- You might notice breast buds, which are small lumps under your nipples. They can be a bit tender, so don't get nervous, it's normal.

Ages 10 to 12: The Changes Kick In

This is when things really start to get noticeable and you might see more changes happening pretty quickly.

- Your breasts will keep growing, and you might start growing pubic hair. (Eeeeeek!) You could also get your first period around this time, but it's totally normal if it comes later.

Ages 12 to 15: Full Speed Ahead

Now you're in the thick of it, with lots of changes happening all at once.

- Your period might be getting more regular around this time. Your body shape will continue developing, but most big changes have already happened.

Ages 15 to 18: The Home Stretch

Several physical changes have happened by this point. You're nearly at the end of your puberty journey.

- You're reaching your adult height and your body is settling into its new shape. Your emotional and social views might change as you get more comfortable in your grown-up body and mind.

How Fast Is All of This Going to Happen?

Puberty doesn't hit the accelerator at the same time for everyone. Some of us breeze through these changes quickly, while others take a more scenic route.

And hey, if you're feeling overwhelmed by how fast or slow things are going, it's cool to talk about it. Whether it's with your parents, a trusted adult, or even your friends, talk it out. Chances are, your friends are puzzling through their own puberty too.

Even though puberty can feel like a wild ride, it's packed with exciting new experiences. You're on your way to becoming the incredible adult you're meant to be. So buckle up and enjoy the changes! Every rollercoaster has its ups and downs, but they all lead to new adventures!

ACTION TAKEAWAYS:

- Breast buds are the first clue that your puberty is beginning.
- Everybody's puberty development is different. Some people start early, and some start late. Whenever you start puberty is exactly the right time for your body.
- Besides the physical changes, your emotions and social views also start shifting as you grow more comfortable with your new adult body and mind.
- Puberty doesn't happen overnight. It's a gradual process. Puberty has its ups and downs, but all those twists and turns lead to the incredible person you're becoming!

4. But, I Don't Want to Grow Up

One second you're the ruler of the playground owning that four square game, and then—Boom!—your body starts changing, your period kicks in, and you get all these social signals that everyone expects you to grow up overnight.

Real Talk: Slow Your Roll

You might feel like you've just zoomed from being a kid to being a grown-up overnight, but guess what? It doesn't really happen like that. Maybe you're excited with the *thought* of growing up, but a period? That wasn't exactly on your wishlist, was it? It's like you want to slam that pause button and stay in Kid-Land a bit longer. I totally get it. You're not alone, and yup, it's totally normal.

I know, I know, hearing something is normal doesn't fix it, but it just lets you know that you're not an alien. You're a real human being going through real human things, and you need to hear that you are normal.

The Struggle is Real

Does it feel like everything is zipping by super fast? Are you feeling rushed? It might seem like going through puberty is your one-way ticket out of your sweet childhood, but no, it's really just a heads up: Things are changing and you're about to start some new awesome adventures in this thing called life.

So, deep breath time—inhale… exhale... pause… Got it? Awesome!

PERSONAL SIDE STORY:

When I was growing up, I felt like I was stuck in this weird place between being a kid and getting older. One minute, I was all about watching cartoons on TV and building epic forts with my little brother, and the next, I was thinking about high school and all these grown-up things that suddenly seemed to matter.

It was like my brain couldn't decide what it wanted. Sometimes I wanted to stay a kid forever, where my biggest worry was whether my favorite show was on. But then other times, I would catch myself thinking about what would come in the future. Who was I going to be? What was I going to do with my life? It was kind of exciting, but also kind of frightening.

And what about all the changes? (Eeeeek!) One day I looked in my bathroom mirror and noticed my face looked different. Not bad, just more grown up. There were all these little zits on my forehead and my breasts were starting to pop out. I thought, "Hey, what's going on here?!" It's like my body was playing some kind of giant prank on me.

But, what was really strange was how sometimes I felt like I was ready to take on the world—like, "Yeah, I've got this!" And then other days, I just wanted to curl up with my stuffed animals and pretend that none of this was happening. It was hard to accept that I couldn't be a kid forever, even though part of me really wanted to.

It was like I was on this crazy carnival ride feeling like I didn't have a seatbelt and no control as to when it would end. And honestly, that was kind of scary. But I figured that's what growing up was, a mixture of excitement and confusion, with a little bit of fear thrown in just for fun.

To be honest, even now, I'm still figuring it out. **Change is a lifelong thing.** But back then, sometimes I was okay with growing up, and other times I kind of wasn't. It was a struggle, but I finally started realizing that maybe it was okay to feel both feelings at the same time. Growing up was weird, but in my heart, I knew everything was going to be okay, and it was.

Here's Your New Mantra:

Say this with me, **"Learning everything all at once is impossible. I'm going to be patient with myself during this big change."**

Now you say it. Go ahead, I'll wait…

What's a Mantra?

A mantra is like a special word or phrase that you say over and over to help you feel calm and focused. Mantras are sort of like magic words that can make you feel better and more confident when you repeat them over and over. For example, saying "I can do this!" before a big test can help you feel brave and focus on doing your best.

Whew! You Did It! First Step, Baby!

Okay, you beautiful thing, remember how you didn't nail soccer your first try? Exactly. It took a bit of time to learn how to not trip over the ball and get the hang of all the rules, right? Getting the hang of your period and puberty is the same way. You'll need a little time to get used to it and figure everything out. So, let's be chill and patient with ourselves during this process.

These Changes Can Be Weird

Sure, your body is pulling some new tricks out of its hat, and yeah, they can feel kind of weird. But all this stuff—like growing taller, dealing with periods, and all those new curves —it's just your body's high-five to you saying everything is moving along just right.

But here's the exciting part: There are some pretty awesome perks and new skills you'll get as you grow from a cool kid into an even cooler adult.

Unlock Your Super Power

As you level up from cool kid to a cooler teen to the coolest adult, you're going to notice some sweet upgrades:

- **New Freedoms:** Handling your period and the whole puberty thing like the superstar you are means you're ready for more adventure and responsibility. More choices, more learning, and taking on exciting challenges. Game on!
- **Super Strength:** Thanks to your handy new hormones like estrogen, you're getting stronger every month. It's like getting a superhero upgrade you didn't know you signed up for!

Think back to those soccer skills we were just talking about. Because of your puberty hormones, you can become stronger on the field by building more muscle and stronger bones.

Your Exciting Future Awaits

Every step in growing up offers more opportunities for you to discover how amazing you can be. And don't worry, growing up doesn't mean leaving all the fun behind. It means adding more amazing chapters to the book of YOU. Sure, it might look a little scary now, but think of all the amazing adventures ahead.

The Journey Continues

Starting your period and rolling through puberty changes are just part of your incredible journey. Each step you take doesn't mean losing anything. What it really means is that you're gaining more power, more wisdom, and more experience!

ACTION TAKEAWAYS:

- Nobody learns everything all at once.
- Puberty will help you become stronger, both physically and mentally.
- Even though puberty can feel overwhelming, it is full of exciting new milestones on your path to becoming an awesome adult!

5. Curves Are Cool!

As you begin to grow up, you'll notice that your body is starting to pull out some new moves. Suddenly, curves start popping out here and there in places that were just flat last week. It's totally normal and kind of cool when you think about it. It's like your body is a secret sculptor working on its new masterpiece! So yeah, you're now transforming into your new super awesome grown-up shape!

What's Happening?

As you cruise through the tween years, your body kicks off some major construction work. Like I mentioned before, you might spot some breast buds popping out around ages 8 to 10. Those are the early birds of puberty, letting you know your body got the memo to start growing up. They might be a little tender, but no worries, it's all part of your body's grand plan.

Breast Buds and Beyond

Breast buds? Yep, they're your chest's way of saying, "Let's get this puberty started!" At first, they're just little bumps, but give them some time, and you'll see even more changes. One day, your chest is flat, and then—Boom!—things start popping! They're like the first domino to tip over, and soon, your period will knock at your door, too.

Breast development is not an overnight thing. It can take a few years for your breasts to fully develop. And guess what? No two are the same. One breast might grow faster than the other at first, which is completely normal and natural.

Embracing Your New Unique You!

Every girl's growth game is different. Some breasts might be round, some might be pointy, but they all grow at their own pace. And hey, if you're comparing yourself to your friends' development, just remember, being different is what makes us all super cool!

Time For a Bra? Yes, Please!

So cool!! It's time to get your first bra! This is a big step! A bra can help support your growing breasts and make you feel more comfortable, especially when you're running and playing sports. A bra is like a trusty sidekick—it supports you and keeps you comfy, especially when you're out saving the world (or just running in gym class).

Let's Get Measured!

Okay, since we're talking bras (No, they're not full-on bras. They are more like baby starter bras), we need to start at the beginning with

Curves Are Cool!

training bras. These bras are like the starter pack; the rookie team in the world of bras. Figuring out your fit can actually be kind of fun (and maybe a little awkward, but hey, that seems to be the norm of things right now). So, let's get going!

A. Check Yourself Out!

Stand in front of a mirror and ask yourself:

- Are your breast buds starting to show through your shirts?
- Do your T-shirts feel tight, or like, weird across your chest?
- Do you just want a training bra because you think it's cool? (Also valid, by the way!)

If you said "yes" to any of these, then yep, it's time!

B. Grab a Tape Measure

No, not the giant metal one from your dad's toolbox! Use the soft, floppy one from your mom's sewing kit (or buy one at the store).

- **Step One:** Wrap the tape snugly around your chest, right under your buds (where the bottom of the bra would sit). This number will be your bra band size. Write down that number. Bra Size Step One # => _____.
- **Step Two:** Now, measure around the fullest part of your chest. You want to go over your breast buds, but not so tight that you're mashing them in. This part might feel a little funny, so just breathe and get it done. Write that number down, too. Step Two # => _____.

C. Math Time! (Don't Worry, It's Easy!)

Subtract the first number, the Bra Size number (under your chest) from the Step Two number (over your chest). Step Two # - Step One # => _____.

- If the difference is 0 to 1 inch: You're a AA.
- If the difference is 1 to 2 inches: You're an A.

That's it! Easy math, no calculators required. These A's and AA's are "cup" sizes. You will need this size code when you go to the store. Now you know your bra size and your cup size! Congrats, you're ready to go shopping!

When you see the salesperson at the store, you'll say something like, "I'm a 32 A" or "I'm a 28 AA." Whatever you figured out above, that's what you'll tell the salesperson! Yayyyyyyyy! (Or just have her measure you!)

D. Shopping Spree! The Bra Treasure Hunt

Now that you know your size, grab your mom and go to the store! When you're shopping for a bra, it's like going on a big treasure hunt for the perfect fit. It needs to feel comfortable, but also have great support. Training bras come in ALL the fun patterns, colors, rainbows, hearts, puppies, and even glittery ones! Some are stretchy pullovers, and others have cute little hooks in the back. (You can't go wrong either way.)

PRO TIP: Go for soft, comfy fabrics. Your chest is still growing, so no need for anything fancy or squishy.

E. Test Drive It

Try it on at home with a T-shirt and make sure:

- It doesn't feel tight or itchy.
- It shouldn't sag or pinch.
- It stays put and doesn't ride up when you reach for the top shelf (a.k.a., the secret candy stash).

If it passes the test, congrats! You're officially in the training bra club!

F. Own It!

This time in your life isn't necessarily about *"needing"* a bra. It's about what makes you feel comfortable and confident. Wear it, rock it, and then laugh when your bestie says, "Wait, does this mean we're grown ups now?!" (Spoiler alert: Not quite, but you're on your way!)

So there you have it, future bra trailblazer! Go forth and slay your training bra adventures!

PERSONAL SIDE STORY:

The day finally came—my first bra shopping trip! I had been feeling like it was time, especially since I noticed some of my friends were already wearing them. But still, the whole thing made me a little nervous. I mean, it's not like they teach you this stuff in school, right?

My mom took me to this store that had about a million different types of bras. Seriously, it was like a whole new world I didn't even know existed. There were lacy ones, sporty ones, colorful ones, and even these tiny little things called training bras. I just stood there, kind of overwhelmed, like, "Uh, where do I even start?"

My mom must have noticed I was having a bit of a freakout. She smiled and said, "Don't worry, we'll find the perfect one for you." She started showing me the different styles, explaining what each one was for, and I realized that getting a bra wasn't as scary as I thought. She even held up a super big-cup bra to my (sort of flat) chest, and we both had a good giggle about it. Those giant cups were something to look forward to, for sure, but it was definitely toooooo early! Hahaha!

We finally found a few that looked comfortable, and I went to try them on. That's when things got real. I put on the first one and looked in the mirror, and I have to admit, it felt kind of weird at first. But then I thought, "Okay, this isn't so bad. I even kind of like it!" It was like a little milestone (one of those things that makes you feel like you're growing up).

After a few tries, I finally decided on a training bra, and it fit perfectly. It wasn't too tight, and it wasn't too loose—just like Goldilocks. It was *just right*. I walked out of the dressing room with a big smile, feeling a mix of excitement and relief. Mom gave me a thumbs up, and I knew she was proud of me.

When we got home, I couldn't wait to show my best friend. She was super excited for me and said, "Welcome to the club!" We giggled about it, and I realized that getting my first bra wasn't just about the bra itself. It was about taking one more step into this whole new world of growing up.

So, getting my first bra was a little nerve-racking, but in the end, it was kind of awesome. It was just one of those things that makes you feel a bit more grown-up, and that's pretty cool.

Change is Cool!

Watching your body as it changes is like starring in your own movie… things are starting to get interesting! It might feel weird, but weird can be exciting! Everyone grows at their own wacky pace and it's perfect to be right where you are.

Wear What Makes You Feel Great

Enjoy these changes by wearing what feels great and fits your style. Clothes can boost your confidence, especially when you notice your body's new look. Find outfits that make you feel great and show off your new outline. Another shopping trip with mom? Yes again, please! Having a nice time with Mom and getting a couple of cool new outfits—you're golden!

Should I Stuff My Bra?

Hmmmm... people have been asking this question ever since bras were created. Sounds scratchy, right? Imagine starting your day with a perfectly puffed up bra, only to find that sneaky toilet paper has wiggled its way up and is peeking out the top of your shirt by lunchtime. (Yikes!) Plus, it's probably not tricking anyone. What if your classmates notice and shout it out? Total embarrassment! (UGH.)

Really, the only reason someone might try this trick is if they're trying to look like someone else. We're going to go over the pitfalls of comparing ourselves to others a bit later in the book, but let me just say, "Uh, no."

Talk It Out

If you ever have questions or are just curious, talk with someone you trust, like your mom, a cool aunt, or even your doctor. They can help you get through these new chapters in your life and make sure you feel comfortable with all the changes.

Remember, You Are Amazing!

Your breasts are just one part of your awesome story of becoming you. Rock your journey with confidence. Know that every change is a step towards becoming the incredible person you're meant to be. Let's celebrate every part of this wild, wonderful ride called puberty!

And, don't stuff your bra with toilet paper. It's scratchy, and honestly, you're fabulous just the way you are. Celebrate your natural self and keep shining, superstar!

ACTION TAKEAWAYS:

- Breast development starts with breast buds. They might be tender.
- You don't want the bra to pinch or sag.
- Get new clothes that make you smile and look great with your new form.
- Got questions? Talk it out!

6. What's Happening to My Face?

Oh No! Acne!

Man, oh man, I wish this was not a thing, but it is. **ACNE** is like one of those annoying party crashers that shows up just when you're starting to feel good about growing up. It's those pimples and zits that pop out on your face and sometimes even on your back and chest. (Yikes, I know!)

They show up when you hit puberty because your body produces more oils (Blecck!), combined with dead skin cells (Aaaargh!), and they clog up your pores (Uuggh!). Plus, all the new hormones racing around in your body can make your skin break out (Help!).

But never fear! Taking care of your face doesn't have to be complicated or take forever each day. Here's what I do:

Washing Your Face

1. Start by washing your face <u>twice a day</u> with a gentle cleanser. Not just soap and water, but wash with something made for faces and acne, especially if you have pimples and blackheads.
2. Use warm (not hot) water to help open up the pores.
3. Be gentle! You can actually make acne worse by scrubbing too hard and irritating your skin. I recommend using only your fingers to wash and rinse your face, but some people like to use a washcloth or an ultra-soft cosmetic brush. Make sure that these tools are clean each time you use them. Bacteria can hide in washcloths, towels, skin brushes and other tools, and it can make your acne worse. Plus, your fingers are so smooth and gentle, perfect for washing your face.
4. After washing, pat your face dry with a clean towel instead of rubbing it.

Besides washing your face regularly, pay attention to what your skin needs.

<u>If Your Skin Is Oily</u>:

Consider using a toner along with a special oil-free moisturizing sunscreen (SPF 30+) that doesn't clog your pores.

You want to look for the term **NON-COMEDOGENIC,** which is either printed **on the front or the back of the bottle. This means "won't clog your pores or cause pimples."**

<u>If Your Skin Is Dry</u>:

Find an oil-free moisturizing sunscreen (SPF 30+) that is hydrating but still light, with the words **<u>NON-COMEDOGENIC</u>**. Once again, this means "won't clog your pores or cause pimples."

SPF stands for Sun Protection Factor, and it lets you know how well the sunscreen you're using will protect your skin from UVA and UVB rays (those are the ones that burn you). If you have fair (light) skin, you'll need an even higher SPF because your skin is super sensitive to the sun. I recommend nothing less than SPF 30, but I would really like to see you using SPF 50 or higher.

NOTE: Use NON-sunscreen moisturizers for nighttime use.

SUGGESTED ROUTINE:

- *Morning*: After you wash your face in the morning, apply that moisturizing sunscreen with at least SPF 30.
- *Nighttime*: After you wash your face at night, make sure that you follow it up with a light moisturizer that does NOT have an SPF factor.

Don't Pop Those Pimples!

Eeeeeek! No matter how tempting it is, don't pop your pimples. It can push that pimple gunk deeper into your skin and even lead to scars. Taking care of your skin now will help it stay clear and happy so you can feel more confident.

BONUS PRO TIP:

If you have a giant zit that won't go away, try this emergency idea. Have one of your parents stop by the drugstore or store and pick up a tube of **WHITE toothpaste, Salicylic Acid, or Benzoyl Peroxide (preferably a paste, not a gel or lotion).** Regarding the toothpaste, make sure it is NOT the gel kind but the *old-school* kind that looks like a white paste. Once you get it, wash your face really well with your regular cleanser, pat it dry, and put a small blob of paste on the big zit only, not on the skin surrounding the zit. Let it sit there for a long time, like an hour. Yes, I said hour! Hide out in your room if you have to! This trick may help dry out the gunk inside the zit below the skin line and also sort of sterilizes the little "infection" brewing below the surface that is creating the zit. Only try it on one pimple first, and see how your skin reacts. DO NOT put the paste all over your face. It will irritate your skin and turn your face red with a rash! (Aaargh!) You don't want a red face or irritation! This is only for occasional use on a giant zit. It doesn't work for everyone, so good luck! I hope it works for you!

Sun Safety—*No Such Thing as a Safe Tan!*

Did you know chilling in the sun without protection is seriously risky for your skin? Yep, that golden tan looks cool, but there's actually no such thing as a safe tan. Let's talk about how you can enjoy the sun safely without turning your skin into a crispy critter.

Sunscreen is Your Bestie

First up, sunscreen is a must. Not just any sunscreen, but one with a high SPF. Choose sunscreens that feel good on your skin. I recommend a moisturizing sunscreen. Try a few brands until you find one that feels good on your face. Once again, everyone's skin is different.

Face SPF Sunscreen vs. Body SPF Sunscreen—Aren't They the Same?

Let's talk about sunscreen. We've got a face SPF sunscreen and we've got body SPF sunscreen, and believe me, they are NOT the same. What if your fancy shoes and go-to sneakers got switched? Just like that, face and body sunscreen each have their own uses.

Face SPF is like the VIP for your face. It's lightweight, non-greasy, and often plays nice with your acne-fighting products. It won't clog your pores or make your face feel like it's got a layer of peanut butter smeared on it. It sometimes has extra goodies like antioxidants or a hint of tint to keep you looking fresh.

Body SPF, on the other hand, is the powerhouse for the rest of your skin. It's thicker, more powerful, and ready to protect your arms, legs, and everything in between from the sun's harsh rays. It's designed to spread easily over large areas, so you're not spending a long time rubbing it in.

So, when you're getting ready for a sunny adventure, or just an everyday moment, remember to grab the right sunscreen for the job. Your face and your body will thank you for the tender loving care.

Reapply Like a Pro

Slapping on sunscreen isn't just a once-and-done deal. You've got to reapply it every couple of hours. And if you're diving into the pool or catching waves at the beach, you need to put it on again as soon as you towel and dry off. Water washes away sunscreen, and even the "water-resistant" types don't stick around forever.

GREAT IDEA!

If you think you might forget to reapply sunscreen, set alarms on your phone, or ask your parents or your friends to remind you.

Dress For Sun Success

Bringing the right clothes can be a game-changer. Choose outfits that cover more skin—think long sleeves and long pants. They're like a cool barrier against the sun's rays. And don't forget a hat. Hats with a wide brim aren't just stylish, they're the shield for your face, ears, and neck from getting burned.

Drink A Lot of Water!

Can I say this enough??? Hahaha! Water is so good for your skin! Try to drink four regular water bottles (16.9-ounce each), or at least 8 cups per day.

Before You Step Out

Develop the habit of wearing sunscreen every time you go outdoors. Even on cloudy days, UV rays can sneak through the clouds and do damage. You won't believe it, but yep, even some indoor lighting can cause UV damage to your skin. Whether it's sunny or overcast, inside or outside, moisturizing sunscreen is your friend.

Watch Out for Sneaky Sun Reflection

- **Reflections From the Sand:** Hanging out at the beach? Being on the sand can make the sun's rays even stronger because it *reflects* sunlight. That means you could get burned even if you're just chilling under an umbrella. More sunscreen, sun-protective clothing, a cool hat, and a shady spot are your best bets for keeping sun-safe.
- **Reflections on a Boat:** Wow, you get to go on a boat? Lucky you! However, another place where you can get damaging sun reflection is on a boat. You might be under a giant hat and a shady overhang, and still get a really bad sunburn. All those sparkly glares of light on that rippling ocean are the sun reflecting onto your face and body. Once again,

What's Happening to My Face?

sunscreen, a sun hat, good sunglasses, and protective clothing are a must.

The next time you plan a day out in the sun, gear up with sunscreen, the right clothes, UV sunglasses, and a stylish hat. Bringing your A-game in protecting your skin is super important. It keeps you healthy and prevents serious stuff like sunburn and other skin problems in the future.

IMPORTANT:

Ignoring sunscreen now may even cause skin cancer when you're an adult. YIKES! The capital "C" word (Seriously, oh no!) let that sink in a moment... Yes, it's real, so treat it like it's real. Wear that sunscreen, my fiend!

So go out there and rock that sunscreen, find some shade, and enjoy the sun safely!

ACTION TAKEAWAYS:

- Acne is a thing, so we need to deal with it. Begin by washing your face twice a day.
- Go shopping for a moisturizing face wash, a non-comedogenic moisturizer, and a moisturizing sunscreen of at least SPF 30 or higher.
- Go shopping for sun-protective clothing: A wide-brim hat, good sunglasses with sun protection, and some protective pants and shirts.
- If you have a really large zit, try the toothpaste, Salicylic Acid, or Benzoyl Peroxide trick. Maybe it will work for you!
- There is no such thing as a safe tan. Serious issues can happen with your skin when you're an adult if you don't use sunscreen now and always. So PLEASE, play in the sun safely by using these sun safety tips.

- Use SPF 30 or higher regularly and reapply often. Set a timer or ask your parents to remind you if you think you might forget to reapply.
- Be aware of sneaky reflective UV rays. They can burn you even when you're standing under shade.

7. Growth Spurts!

Have you ever felt like you went to bed one size and woke up another? One day your pants fit, and the next day, they're like capris? (Whaaaat?) Super weird, but also totally normal for this time in your life. Every person goes through it, both guys and girls. And that means your body is doing exactly what it's meant to do: **GROW!** You might suddenly feel like your body is stretching faster than cheese on a pizza.

This chapter is about getting to know your body, figuring out what's happening, and totally rocking those changes.

Your Body's Power-up Mode

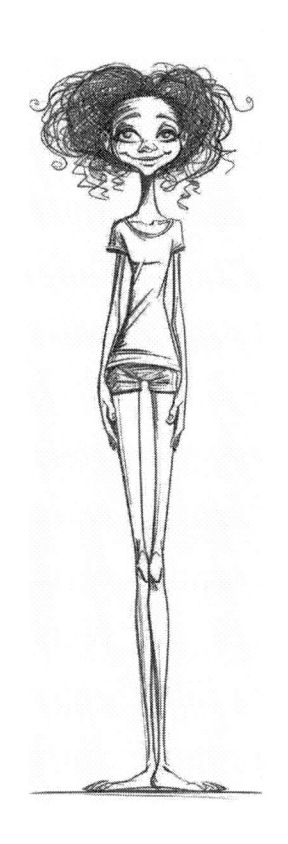

Growth spurts are like your body's version of a super-speed level-up in a video game, and they can feel just as wild. It's natural for your body to suddenly kick into high gear during your teen years. This happens because your body is getting all the right signals from your brain to grow, grow, grow!

If you find yourself eating more or feeling like your shoes are a little tight, it's all part of the plan. You need to get bigger because you don't want to stay like a kid-sized candy bar your whole life, right? All these things are part of the giant plan of growing up.

The Puppy Paw Stage

During these growth spurts, you might feel a bit clumsy or awkward. Like a puppy growing into its paws. Yep, that's you! Your arms and legs are growing faster than the rest of you, making you feel gangly. Don't sweat it though, it's just your body trying to figure out how to handle its new size and strength. It's also a great excuse if you're suddenly tripping over your feet more than usual.

Growing Strong

The coolest part? Your growth spurt is just another step closer to becoming the adult version of you. It's like watching a sneak preview of "You: The Grown-Up Edition." Make sure you're eating right and getting plenty of sleep during these turbo growth times, because your body is doing a ton of work at night to get taller and stronger. And hey, always remember to stretch and stay active. It helps make those growing muscles and bones stay strong and flexible.

ACTION TAKEAWAYS:

- During puberty, it's not uncommon for someone to shoot up a couple of inches in height in a very short period of time.

- As you go through a growth spurt, walking and running might feel awkward. You might feel a bit clumsy because you're not used to your new height.
- Enjoy your new body! Go out and get some new clothes to decorate the new you!

8. Hair? Down There?

As we cruise through this wild adventure called puberty, let's talk about something a little bit fuzzy. Yep, we're talking **HAIR.** Out of nowhere, you'll spot hair in places that were just peachy smooth before.

Yep, your body is going into full beast mode on hair growth! You'll spot new hairs under your arms, on your legs, and yes, even in the VIP areas *"down there."* It's all part of turning into a grown-up.

From the Hair on Your Head to Your Cute Tippy Toes

- **Leg Hair Levels Up:** During puberty, your leg hair decides to crank up the volume by getting thicker and darker.
- **Arm Hair Gets an Upgrade:** Not letting your legs have all the attention, your arm hair also gets a bit thicker. It might not be as obvious as leg hair, but it's just doing its thing, keeping you warmer and protected.

- **What's Up with My Head Hair?** Your scalp might get oilier, making your head feel a bit greasy. That oily feeling is created because your glands are in overdrive, thanks to puberty. Switch up your shampoo routine to keep the greasy look away.
- **Underarm Hair Enters the Chat:** Your underarm hair is now making its grand debut. It starts off shy with just a few soft hairs and then gets thicker and curlier as it sets in.
- **And Then There's Pubic Hair:** Yep, we're going there—pubic hair. (Gaaaaah!) It starts off soft and thin but gets thicker and curlier as you grow. Its job is to keep your private areas clean by trapping dirt and other stuff.
- **Huh? Hair On My Big Toes?** Yup, surprise! Even your big toes might join the hair party. Yeah, even those little piggies might need a little comb soon. Who knew, right? Hahahaha!

To Shave or Not to Shave?

Ahhhh, the big question! Whether you save or not is totally up to you. Some people shave because they like feeling smooth, or maybe it's a sports thing. But hey, if you're not into shaving, that's cool, too.

- **The Good and the Not So Good:** Shaving can make you feel sleek and smooth, but it can be a hassle. Watch out for that sneaky stubble and the annoying razor burn.
- **Pressure to Shave:** Everyone, from ads in magazines to your friends at school, has an opinion on shaving. But, whether you shave or not is completely your choice.

Your Body, Your Rules

Whether you rock the soft hairy look or go silky smooth, what matters is how good you feel in your own skin. Puberty is about figuring out you, and every choice helps you learn more about yourself.

If you're curious about shaving, chat with your parent, an older sibling, or someone else you trust to show you the ropes safely. A personal demonstration is the best way to learn.

Whatever your hair decision is, own it with confidence. Your body is doing exactly what it's supposed to be doing during this wild ride called puberty, and that's totally something to be proud of.

So, rock what you got, and enjoy the ride!

ACTION TAKEAWAYS:

- Heads up! You're going to grow more hair just about everywhere!
- Deciding to shave is completely up to you.
- DO NOT buy cheap no-name razors because you'll wind up with a lot of cuts and razor burn.
- Shaving? Only YOU decide what's right for your body.

9. Welcome to the Period Club!

You've probably heard about getting your **PERIOD,** right? It's like a monthly meeting that every girl will attend at some point. So, let's break it down—what a period is, what to expect, and how to handle it like a champ!

BONUS PRO TIP:

Grab a copy of ***MY PERIOD POWER!*** It's a <u>PERIOD</u> CONFIDENCE GUIDE, the companion book to this one that is your go-to guide packed with everything you need to know about your period life. What we're covering here? Just a sneak peek!

You'll also want to get the ***MY PERIOD POWER! WORKBOOK,*** to help you on your period journey. It will help you track and monitor your period so that you can predict when it starts, plus it includes recipes, fun puzzles, coloring pages and special insight. They are essential in knowing the ins and outs of all things period!

A Brief History of Your Body From the Beginning

Let's think of it this way—when a baby girl is still growing inside her mom, her body sets up hormones and future egg cells almost at the same time. Her body is getting ready for the big show that won't happen until she's much older, like when she hits puberty.

- **Egg Cells (Eggs):** These special cells are the VIP guests for an event planned for far into the future. Every girl is born with all the egg cells she will ever have. They're just hanging out, not doing much, waiting for this gigantic event: Puberty. This is when the body says, "Okay, it might be time to get one of these VIPs ready each month." But just know, these VIP guests were on the guest list from the very start, even before a girl was born.
- **Hormones:** These are the signals or messages that run everything, telling different parts of your body what to do and when. Some hormones are around doing basic jobs, even when a girl is just a baby. But the major work, like causing periods to start and making it possible for you to have a baby, doesn't kick off until puberty. That's when the hormones really start ramping up their activity, getting everything ready for the monthly party where an egg takes the spotlight and says, "Hello World!"

Okay, the history lesson is o-ver!

What's Up With Puberty and That First Period?

It seems as if this is a crazy carnival ride your body goes on without asking you first. One day, you're chilling, and the next, you've got boobs growing, hair sprouting in strange places, and yeah, that thing called a period.

It might feel weird and sometimes totally unfair since guys don't have a period. Yes, I can be a challenge when you have to handle it at school and during sleepovers. But trust me, it's all part of the awesome (kind of annoying) journey of growing up.

Everybody's period experience is different. That first period (menarche) is like a badge of honor, and how you react to it will be totally your own experience. There is no right or wrong way of reacting. You do you, baby! Be proud!

No matter how or when it happens to you, just know that you're not alone. Every girl has been there or will be at some point. And this book? It's here to make sure you're smiling, learning, and readying yourself on how to tackle this puberty thing head-on.

You'll grow taller. Your body will change shape. You'll get curvier. You might get zits (pimples). You might even feel moodier than usual. Does any of this sound familiar to you? If so, CONGRATULATIONS! You're probably going through puberty right now, and that's the reason you got this book!

Understanding Puberty, Your Body and Your Period

It doesn't matter what body type you are, puberty will find you! Whether you are tall, short, skinny, or round, your body is perfect for you, and I'm even going so far as to say that it's beautiful! You can even go into the bathroom right now, look in the mirror and say (or scream!) "I'M BEAUTIFUL!" Heehee! I love it! Yeah, go ahead, I'll wait!

If you have any doubts about the incredibleness of your body, get those thoughts out of your head right now. Your body is an amazing machine. If you give it food, rest, and a little love, it will last you many, many years. Sure, every once in a while, we need to take it to the mechanic, but mostly, it's a finely tuned machine that literally billions of people have test-driven over many centuries!

The Science of Menstruation (Seriously, It's Not Rocket Science)

Inside your belly, you've got these two things called ovaries and they're like tiny egg factories. Every month, they drop an egg, and your body says, "Let's get this place ready in case we're having a baby!" That's when the walls of your uterus get all cozy and soft.

But when no baby shows up, your body says, "Okay, party's over," and it gets rid of all that cozy stuff. That's what menstruation (your period) is—it cleans house and makes everything fresh again. It's a little yucky and sometimes be a pain (literally), but it's your body doing its natural thing, making sure that everything is working A-OK.

The whole "cycle" lasts about a month—one week with your period and then three weeks without. It's your very own monthly subscription, except you didn't sign up for it, and there's no cancel button (bummer, I know). It can vary by a few days, especially in the beginning. But when you get older, your periods will probably become pretty regular and you can pretty much anticipate exactly when your period will start each month.

In every cycle, your hormones are going up and down. Hormones are behind the scenes, making sure the egg cell gets released (ovulation) and then telling your uterus to get ready just in case a baby starts growing. It's a lot of work your female parts are doing each month.

No baby? No problem! Your body just hits the reset button (a.k.a. your period), and the whole cycle starts over.

Dealing With Those Crazy Period Symptoms

Now, let's talk about the stuff that can make your period a little difficult. Cramps, for starters. They range from "Oh, that's annoying" to "Why, oh why can't I just stay in bed all day?" Cramps happen because your uterus is contracting (basically squeezing its muscles) to help shed its lining. Imagine your uterus trying to win a gold medal in gymnastics right inside your tummy. Sometimes, not so fun.

Then there are the mood swings. One minute you're laughing, and the next you're crying because your sock won't go on right. It's all thanks to those wild hormone ups and downs. And, let's not forget the cravings—chocolate, potato chips, you name it. It's like your body thinks it's going on a deserted island and needs all the snacks NOW!

PERSONAL SIDE STORY:

Let's just say I wasn't thrilled to join the period club right before I had to go to ballet class. Having to wear pink tights and a leotard! (Aaaaargh!) I wanted my period to start for so long because all my friends already had theirs. But when the moment finally came, I thought I was going to faint! I saw stars, girl! I had to sit down… the room was spinning. Was this really happening? I called my mom, and she started crying, so happy that I was becoming a woman. "Ugh, thanks Mom." *(Click!)*

Your Period Product Cheat Sheet

Pads, tampons, menstrual cups, oh my! Choosing what to use can feel like trying to pick a favorite ice cream flavor.

- **Pads** are like the comfy sweats of period products; no fuss, just stick them in your undies and go.
- **Tampons?** They're sort of like skinny jeans. They take a bit of getting used to, but are super for swimming or running.
- **Menstrual cups** are like those high-tech sneakers. They're sort of intimidating at first, but once you get the hang of them, they're game changers.

Shopping for Supplies

Hit the period aisle in the store, and pick your potion: Pads, tampons, or menstrual cups. Pads are great for first-timers, and will also be your go-to for a lot of your period life. You change pads every 4 to 8 hours, depending on how heavy your flow is. For tampons, you must change them every 4-6 hours max.

<u>VERY IMPORTANT:</u>

NEVER leave a tampon in longer than six hours! You could develop a serious bacteria party inside your body called **Toxic Shock Syndrome (TSS)**—which is <u>super serious</u>. **<u>SIX HOURS MAX!</u>**

The First Time

When the day comes, it might be a mix of "yay!" and "yikes!" The color could range from light pink, bright red, or even a bit brownish. Those are all typical colors.

Caught off guard without a pad or a tampon?

Don't panic! Just fold some toilet paper and place it in your underwear, and then find a trusted adult, friend, or older sister to help you out with some supplies.

Trash Talk

Done with your pad or tampon? Wrap it up like a little burrito in toilet paper or in its original wrapper and throw it away in the trash. NEVER FLUSH IT down the toilet because it can cause major clogs, and your parents will be very unhappy with you! VERY!

How Long? How Often?

Do you think it's gonna be a flood? No way! It's only about three tablespoons throughout your entire period. That's about the same as three ketchup packets. Not so scary now, huh?

It can last as few as 3 days and as many as 8 days and rolls around every 25 to 40 days. Normally, it lasts about 6-8 days. And getting into a rhythm? It might take a while for your period to get on a regular schedule, but that's okay.

You're a Woman Now

Yup, you heard that right! (Eeeeek!) Your body is doing womanly things, and beginning your period also means that IF you become sexually active (which means sexual intercourse) with a member of the opposite sex, you could get pregnant.

IMPORTANT:

Let's state that again because it's really important: <u>You could get pregnant</u>.

Now, considering that this is a book about getting your first period, getting to know how your body functions, and everything that goes along with this beautiful transition into adulthood, having intercourse and getting pregnant is probably not on your immediate list of things to do. However, you need to be aware that the possibility of pregnancy is a real situation if you are sexually active and have sexual intercourse.

We're not really going to cover sex or pregnancy topics in detail in this book because that's a very large subject with a lot of personal (and maybe even religious) decisions you need to make. However, it is something that you need to know. When the time is right later in your development, you will want to talk about it with your parents and your doctor <u>BEFORE</u> becoming sexually active.

It is never too soon to have real conversations like these with the people you trust to give you good advice and guidance.

You've Got This!

Here's the thing, your periods might seem like the worst thing ever, especially when you're trying to figure out how to take some control over them. But you need to listen to me here —you're stronger than you think. Together with this book, we're going to tackle all the weird, awkward, and, yes, even the cool parts of puberty.

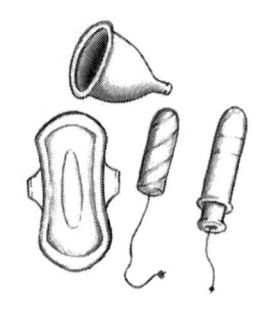

Remember, every period journey is unique, but one thing is for sure— we're all in this together. So, grab your munchies and your cozy robe, and let's dig in! You and me together, we've got this!

And who knows? By the end of ***MY BODY POWER!, MY PERIOD POWER!*** and ***MY PERIOD POWER! WORKBOOK,*** you might not be in *love* with your period, but at least you'll be armed with all the knowledge, tips, and tricks to deal with it like a boss.

ACTION TAKEAWAYS:

- Eggs and hormones are there from the beginning.
- Start looking in the stores or online for pads, tampons, and menstrual cups.
- Make sure you get my other books, ***MY PERIOD POWER!, MY SOCIAL POWER!,*** the ***MY SOCIAL POWER! WORKBOOK,*** and the ***MY PERIOD POWER! WORKBOOK,*** to help you on your period journey. They are essential in learning everything about your period!

10. Make a Difference with Your Review

Remember that wild moment when you realized, **"OMG! I'm growing up?"** Your body was changing, your period was around the corner. It was a mashup of *"Yikes, this is new!"* and *"Wow, this is so exciting!"*

Think back to those whispers in the hallway about periods, or when you got that clueless, *"Wait, a tampon goes where???"* moment? Wishing there was a guide that wasn't like a textbook or sounded awkward?

<u>Well, guess what? You can be that guide!</u>
Yup, just like you needed advice, other teens need the same. **You could be the one** who makes them feel less alone, less confused, and way more confident.

Helping others makes you feel like a total superhero. People who lift others up live happier lives, so why not sprinkle that magic everywhere? If we have the chance to help ourselves **and** help others at the same time… well, heck… I think we should try.

Would you spend 60 seconds to make someone's life a little brighter?

1. Tap the link or scan the QR code!

https://dub.sh/ALLA

2. Share your feelings. *How did it help you? Did it make you smile?* Did you have an *"Oh, I get it now!" moment?*

3. Give your **Written Review, Your Stars ★★★★★ Rating, and Submit**, and know that you just helped someone else improve their life in the coolest way possible.

4. **Maybe add a picture or video** of yourself along with your review and online talking about how the book helped you! I'd love to see who you are! **#MyBodyPower!**

It feels good to share the secret sauce of growing up! So, why not be that person?

Your words could totally change someone's life. How cool is that? Thank you for being a part of this mission to spread confidence and a whole lot of body power!

Confidence shared is confidence multiplied. Keep shining, superstar!

Your biggest fan,

SheriBelle Karper

11. Shape and Weight Changes During Puberty

As puberty keeps doing its thing, your body's going to change—A LOT. One day you'll look in the mirror and say, "Wait, when did *this* happen?!" But here's the deal: Your body has its own secret blueprint and knows exactly what to do. Let's look at what's happening and why letting your body do its thing is super important.

Your Body's Blueprint

During puberty, your body goes through a ton of changes. Here's the cool part: It already secretly knows how to get its shape based on your unique genetic code. (Whoa! Am I right?!) This means that everyone's body develops differently based on their family history. It's mind-blowing that your body has the memory code built right into your cells!

You may see your hips getting wider or gaining some weight around your thighs and arms. It's super important to remember that puberty is a time for your body to grow the way it's supposed to, not how a magazine or some Instagram post says it should. Everyone's body is different, and that diversity makes us all special.

Why Dieting Isn't Cool Right Now

With your body changing so much, you might be tempted to slam on the brakes on that eating thing, but don't even think about cutting back. Your body needs fuel to create all this change and muscle growth.

If you try to diet during this time, you might not give your body enough of what it needs to grow properly. Instead of dieting, focus on eating different types of foods that give you energy and make you feel good. Fruits, vegetables, proteins, and yes, even carbs and fats are all part of a healthy diet.

Tune In to Your Body

Your body is constantly sending you signals. Make sure you listen to them!

- If you are hungry, **eat!**
- If you are thirsty, **drink!**
- If you are tired, **get some sleep!**
- If you are dirty, **take a shower!**

And the list goes on, but you get the idea. Seems simple, right? I know all these things seem completely obvious to you, but sometimes we get so caught up in our thoughts that we forget that we can help ourselves in such easy ways if we just listen to our bodies.

Embrace Your Changes

Puberty is a time of change, and every change your body goes through is preparing you for the amazing person you are becoming. So instead of worrying about your shape or your weight, try to focus on what your body can do—like how fast you can run, how high you can jump, or how you can dance like nobody's watching.

If you ever feel unsure or unhappy about how your body is changing, it's really helpful to talk about it. Talk it over with your parents, a trusted teacher, a counselor, or even your doctor. They can remind you of how normal these changes are and help you see how wonderful your body really is.

IMPORTANT:

Your body is your own special space. It is private. This means you get to decide who can get close to you. This includes family, friends, or anyone else. If someone makes you feel weird or uncomfortable—like touching you in a way you don't like—it is very important to talk to an adult you trust right away. **DON'T KEEP IT A SECRET**. And keeping secrets that make you feel bad isn't good for your mental health. Always tell someone if something or someone is bothering you. You are important, and your feelings and well-being matter a lot.

Celebrate Yourself!

As you grow, learn to celebrate your body for what it can do, not just for how it looks. Whether you're into sports, dance, art, or anything else, use your body to express yourself and have fun. After all, these changes are just part of the journey to becoming the awesome person you're meant to be.

So, trust the process, my friend. You are literally under construction!

ACTION TAKEAWAYS:

- During puberty, your body will probably change a lot.
- It's important not to diet during puberty. Your body really needs the calories right now to build the new, fantastic adult-sized you!
- Listen to your body! It's constantly telling you what it needs.
- Your body is private. Do not keep secrets if someone is making you feel uncomfortable or touching you inappropriately.
- Try not to judge your body during this time. It takes a while for puberty to finish. You are a work in progress!

12. What's That Smell?... Body Odor and Care of Your Body

Let's talk about something a bit awkward but super important: **BODY ODOR.** While we're at it, let's talk about body care, as well. Yep, we're in that stinky time of life, and that stink starts kicking in during puberty. Body odor (B.O.) is totally natural and happens to everyone, but let's figure out how to keep it under control so you can stay fresh and confident!

Body Odor: Why Do I Smell Different Now?

During puberty, your body starts producing more hormones, especially one called androgen. These hormones crank up your sweat glands. Now, I could get all *science-y* and list all these big words, but basically, these glands are mainly in your underarms and around your inner thighs. They produce a thicker kind of sweat (Eeuuww!). When this sweat mixes with the bacteria on your skin—Boom!—body odor! (Uuuugh!) Stink-O-Rama!

Good Grooming to the Rescue!

Keeping body odor in check is all about good grooming. Here are some top tips to help you stay smelling like flowers and sunshine!

Shower Power!

Take a shower every day. Yes, I said every day! Use mild soap and wash all over, especially in your underarms and on your feet.

Yes, you also need to wash your coo-koo-la (your *"down there"*) and your butt-crack (Aaaaargh! Did I just say that?!) with soap. Yup, this is an all-important part of keeping yourself fresh. It's time you get acquainted with your body.

IMPORTANT:

Make sure that everything you wash with soap is completely rinsed off with water. If you leave soap on your skin without rinsing, you will feel a burning sensation after a while, and your skin will get irritated. No one wants that!

It's All Part of Growing Up

Developing body odor is just one of the many changes that comes with puberty. It's nothing to be embarrassed about. It happens to everyone, but it's something you can control.

If you're ever unsure about what products to use or how to handle grooming, it's totally okay to ask your parents, older sibling, or a trusted adult for some tips. They've been exactly where you are now and can definitely help you out.

What's That Smell?... Body Odor and Care of Your Body

Let's Get a Plan!

Here are some grooming tips so you'll be ready to tackle body odor head-on!

Wear Clean Clothes:

Make sure you start each day with a fresh set of clothes, especially socks and underwear. Wearing clean clothes not only helps you smell good, but also makes you feel good. If you've had a sweaty day or had gym class, changing your clothes is a smart move.

Washing Your Hair:

As you grow up, you might notice your hair getting kind of greasy. It's what happens sometimes because of changing hormones. To keep it looking and smelling fresh, wash it at least a few times a week. If you're always on the move, if you play sports, or if it's just naturally super oily, you might even want to wash it every day.

Use a gentle shampoo that matches your hair type and don't forget a good conditioner. To combat knotty hair, get a good conditioner that can help detangle and make your hair smoother. This way, you can keep your hair clean and rocking it without a fuss!

Foot Focus

Feet can get really stinky, especially if you wear the same shoes daily. Wash your feet well in the shower, and dry them thoroughly afterward. Wearing socks with your shoes and changing them daily can also help keep the stink away. Maybe use foot powder if your feet are feeling a bit too swampy. And hey, if your shoes start smelling funky, toss in a couple dryer sheets overnight or give them a day or two to air out!

BONUS PRO TIP:

When you need to shower at a public facility, it's best to wear flip-flops or water shoes the entire time you're taking your shower, and even while dressing in the locker area. There are certain fungi and bacteria that can pass on to your feet when you come in contact with flooring in a public area. One of these is Athlete's Foot, and it's a little tough to get rid of. Wearing plastic shoes in the shower (and changing), so that your feet never actually touch the floor is the best way to protect against those fungal infections and bacteria.

Your Ears:

Did you know you can get acne and blackheads inside your ears? (Euuuww!) That's why it's very important to wash your ears every time you shampoo or shower. When your fingers are still sudsy with shampoo, a quick little wash in and behind your ears is usually enough to keep them squeaky clean and free of acne. Afterward, just lean your head sideways onto your towel to get the water out on each side. Gently wipe the outside of your ears with your towel or even a cotton swab. But hey, never ever poke anything pointy inside your ears, not even a cotton swab! You could really hurt your eardrums.

About earwax: You know that gooey yellow stuff inside your ears? It's actually supposed to be there. It helps trap dirt, so it doesn't go deeper into your ears. But if you feel like there's too much wax, that it's making it so that you can't hear very well, or your ears feel all plugged up, talk with your parents or a doctor to figure out a safe way to get it cleaned out. If the inside of your ears ever feels painful, or if you're losing your balance, you might have an ear infection. If so, it is important to have your parents get you to a doctor to see what they can do for it.

Wash Your Tools:

Tools you use in your bathroom (like your brushes and combs) can also get dirty with buildup from using them in your hair. Maybe give them a good wash about every two or three weeks to keep them in tip-top shape. Just use warm, soapy water and rinse them really well. They will be as good as new!

BONUS PRO TIP:

It's a big NO for sharing your comb, brush, mascara, and basically anything else with someone else. Sharing eyeliner or mascara is a fast way to swap germs or even get an eye infection (no thanks!). There are certain diseases, bacteria, and even bugs (Yes! I said bugs called lice! (Aaaargh!)) They can travel through close contact, or by sharing brushes and grooming tools. Lice are very hard to get rid of. (Yikes!) Yeah, don't let that happen to you. Say something like, "Oh, my mom doesn't let me share my stuff. I'm so sorry." Then, it wasn't you that told your friend *"No,"* it was actually your mother. So, it's no problem!

Diet Check:

What you eat can also affect how you smell. Foods like onions, garlic, and strong spices can make your sweat smell stronger. It's good to eat what you like, but if you notice your body odor changes after certain foods, that might be why.

Staying Hydrated:

Drink plenty of water to help get rid of the toxins that also create body odor. Plus, staying hydrated is just a good health tip in general.

Deodorant or Antiperspirant:

After you shower, use deodorant or antiperspirant on your underarms. Deodorant helps *mask* the smell of sweat, while antiperspirant helps *reduce* sweating.

NOTE:

Some deodorants can leave a white mark on clothing. Try to find ones with the word "invisible" printed on the label. Find a scent you like, or go for an unscented type if you're not into smelling like a "tropical breeze" or a "fresh ocean!"

The Eyes Have It!

Hey, did you know it's super important to get your eyes checked out every year? Many kids, especially girls, don't realize they have a vision problem until they're hitting the books hard in school, usually around 3rd to 5th grades.

Spotting the Signs

Do you need glasses? If you're getting headaches a lot, squinting to see stuff far away or close up, or if things look kind of like a double (like there's two of everything), it's definitely time to check in with an eye doctor.

The Lowdown on Eye Exams

Getting your eyes tested isn't just about reading random letters off the eye chart. It's about making sure your eyes are healthy and catching any issues early. Eye doctors are pros at this, and they can totally help you out if things seem a little blurry.

And if you need glasses, you won't be the only one. It's no biggie. Loads of people wear them. Getting fitted for glasses can actually be pretty fun. It's like a little mini makeover! You get to choose frames that match your style. You can choose different shapes or ones with a pop of color.

Glasses, Contacts, and Protection, Oh My!

Not feeling glasses? Contacts might be your thing. They give you clear vision without having to wear glasses all the time, which is perfect if you're super active or in sports.

Speaking of sports, don't forget about protecting your eyes. Whether you're outside soaking up the sun or doing something adventurous like mountain biking, wearing the right eye protection can keep your eyes safe from harm.

Getting your eyes checked isn't just another thing on your to-do list—it's about making sure you can see your world clearly and keep doing all the things you love doing without missing a beat. Whether you're picking out cool new frames, trying new contacts, or rocking some stylish sunglasses, taking care of your eyes is a big deal. Clear vision is your ticket to a clear path ahead, so keep those peepers in check!

Your Smile!

Did you know your smile is like your superpower? It's the first thing people notice, and it's like having an invitation saying, "Hey, come hang out with me!" So, making sure your smile is bright and welcoming is super important. Here's the scoop on keeping your grin looking great and healthy by mastering the art of brushing your teeth.

Why We Brush: The Lowdown on Plaque

First off, why do we even brush? Well, there's this sneaky stuff called plaque—basically a film of bacteria just sitting there chilling on your teeth. (Yuuuck!) Yeah, I said bacteria IN YOUR MOUTH! (Gaaag!) It's kind of the villain in your mouth's story. Letting it hang around can lead to cavities (Ouch!) and gum disease (Double Ouch!)

and eventually tooth loss (Are you kidding me??!! No! I am not!). We brush to kick the plaque to the curb and keep our mouths healthy.

Brushing Basics: Twice a Day Keeps the Cavities Away

So yeah, you've got to brush at least twice a day—once in the morning to kick start your day and once at night to clean off the day's build-up. And, if you can swing it, brushing after each meal is a total win. It's even cool to pack your toothbrush in your backpack or take it to sleepovers. That way, you always have your toothbrush ready for a quick brush, and you won't be tempted to skip a brush.

Picking the Perfect Toothbrush

Choosing the right toothbrush is also key. Go for one with soft bristles and a small head. It's easier on your gums and can reach those tricky spots. Swap out your toothbrush every 2 to 3 months because old brushes just don't do the job right.

Brushing Like a Pro

When you brush, cover all the angles. Brush the front, back, and the tops and bottoms of your teeth, both inside and outside. It's like painting a mini masterpiece twice a day. Make sure you get all those surfaces so the plaque doesn't stand a chance.

Don't Forget to Brush Your Tongue!

Tongue?? Yep, your tongue needs some cleaning love, too. Brushing your tongue helps kick bad breath and clears out the bacteria (More bacteria? Are you kidding me?). Just a quick scrub at the end of your brushing routine can make a big difference.

Make sure you rinse your toothbrush well so it's clean and ready for later!

What's That Smell?... Body Odor and Care of Your Body

Floss Like a Boss

And hey, don't forget to floss! It gets the gunk out from between your teeth, where your brush can't reach. It's like a secret weapon for a total clean.

Keeping up with brushing and flossing is like taking care of your smile superpower. It keeps you ready to greet everyone with confidence and shows the world you're all about staying healthy. So, grab that brush, flash that grin, and show off your awesome smile every chance you get.

Your Gums

All of this starts with keeping your gums healthy, your breath fresh, and hitting up your dentist for regular checkups. Let's figure out how you can keep your mouth game strong.

Gums are like a cozy blanket for your teeth. Keeping them healthy is a big deal because unhealthy gums can lead to many not-so-fun things like gum disease and tooth loss (Holy Crappoly!). And trust me, you don't want that. Brushing gently at the gum line and flossing daily are your best moves to keep your gums in great shape. If they ever start to look red or bleed when you brush, it's time to tell your parents because a dentist checkup might be needed.

Breath That's Fresh as a Mint

Let's talk about fresh breath because no one wants to be the one with "dragon breath." Am I right? Staying on top of your brushing and flossing game is key here, along with brushing your tongue like I said before. It's a major hideout for bacteria that cause awful smells.

Chewing sugar-free gum after meals can also help kick bad breath by increasing saliva, which is nature's way of washing your mouth. Staying hydrated by drinking plenty of water during the day helps wash away food particles and bacteria. Sooooo, buh-bye, bad breath! Buh-bye!

Dentist Visits are Cool, Seriously!

Visiting the dentist might not sound like a thrill ride, but think of it as a pit stop for your smile. Regular checkups, usually every six months, help catch any sneaky problems before they become big deals. Dentists are like detectives for your teeth and mouth. They make sure everything is running smoothly and give you tips on brushing and flossing like a pro. There's also usually a free toothbrush or goodies at the end, so that's a win!

Keeping your teeth brushed, your gums healthy, and visiting your dentist regularly are all part of the magic formula for a dazzling smile. These habits are all part of your daily health routine, just like eating right and getting enough sleep. Your mouth will thank you with a gorgeous smile, and you'll feel great knowing you are taking care of your health. Keep up the good work and show off that grin!

Braces Anyone?

Getting braces is a popular thing, even movie stars and grown-ups rock them! If you're about to join the brace club, you're in awesome company. Millions of people across America are sharing the journey with you. There are even braces that are invisible!!

What's That Smell?... Body Odor and Care of Your Body

Braces Are Cool (Yes, Really!)

Okay, so you might be a tad nervous about what others think. I get it. But here's the thing: Braces are your ticket to a super straight and gorgeous smile down the line in the future. Imagine flashing those perfectly aligned teeth and feeling ultra-confident. You're working on something great right now that later will be something you'll be super proud of!

You're Not Alone If You Have Braces

Remember, you're not the only one dealing with braces. Loads of kids and teens are going through the same thing. When you see someone else with braces, give them a smile! It's like an exclusive club with a super cool secret handshake (but, you know, with smiles).

Brace Brushing: A Little Different Than Regular

With braces, brushing your teeth gets a little more complicated. You'll need to be a bit more careful and thorough. Get an "interproximal brush" from your orthodontist. It will become your new best bud.

It's specially designed to clean around your braces and in between your teeth. Make it your mission to keep those braces sparkly clean!

Watch What You Eat

Yep, there are some food rules when you have braces.

- Hard foods? They're a no-go because they can break your braces.
- Sticky foods? Steer clear from those to avoid a cleaning nightmare.
- Chewy foods? Caramels, fruit chews, and other super chewy

foods—a big NO! They can actually pull your braces off! (Eeeeek!) It's all about keeping your braces safe so they can do their job well.

You Can Still Show Off Your Style

Here's the fun part: You can still totally express yourself with your braces. Every time you visit your orthodontist for a checkup, you can choose new colors for your rubber bands. It's like accessorizing your smile. Go bold, pick seasonal colors, or match them to your mood or outfit. Super fun!

As this chapter closes, with a little effort in grooming, you should be coming out of it smelling like flowers and sunshine! So, keep rocking your awesome body and keep it smelling fresh!

ACTION TAKEAWAYS:

- Buy deodorant or antiperspirant. Have fun choosing a scent that you like.
- Shower daily! Wash your body, shampoo your hair, and rinse completely.
- Wear clean clothes every day.
- Get an eye exam to see if you have any problems.
- Brush your teeth, tongue, and floss every day, twice a day.
- See your dentist twice a year.
- Braces are cool! Make sure you get that special "interproximal brush" from your orthodontist.
- Enjoy your clean body and smile!

13. Eating Well and Feeling Great!

Let's talk about something super important: **EATING!** I mean, Yum! Am I right?! It's not about grabbing whatever snack is closest to you (even though we've all been there). It's about giving your body the fuel it needs to keep you feeling awesome. So, let's break it down and figure out how to keep those meals balanced so that you're not running on chips and hope, but actually giving your body the energy it needs to crush the day!

What's On Your Plate?

Eating a balanced diet means getting a mix of the good stuff:

1. Fruits
2. Vegetables
3. Proteins
4. Grains
5. Dairy

Imagine your plate at mealtime—half of it should be fruits and vegetables, one-fourth should be protein (like chicken, fish, or beans), and the other quarter should be whole grains (like whole wheat or brown rice). And don't forget a serving of dairy, like a glass of milk or a cup of low-fat yogurt.

What's the Dealio with Allergies?

Imagine your body is like a superhero team. It usually fights off the bad guys (like germs) to keep you going at your highest level. But sometimes it gets a bit mixed up, and thinks that foods that are normally good for you—like nuts, dairy, gluten, or shellfish—are out to get you. That's an allergy.

Sometimes, the reactions to allergies are small, like a rash or a puffy tummy full of gas. But other times, the reactions are huge and even kind of dangerous. Either way, we need to listen to our body when it's telling us, "No-Thank-You." It's like having a party, where we have to keep certain party crashers OUT!

Don't Worry, There's Still a Feast!

So, what can you munch on if you've got these food allergies? Lots of things! Living with allergies means you become a label-reading wizard. You'll see words like "gluten-free" or "nut-free" and then you'll do a happy dance because, yes, you can eat it!

Dining Out? No Problemo!

Eating out? Just tell the servers what you need to watch out for, and then they will tell the chefs about your allergies. They're like the guardians of the kitchen, making sure your meal is safe from anything that could mess with you. And always pack your "just in case" gear. Maybe carry an EpiPen or antihistamines if your body has allergic reactions. You need to be prepared!

IMPORTANT:

When the server brings out your food, it's always a good idea to look it over and reconfirm verbally with the server that the chef prepared it the way you need it. Better *safe* than *sorry!*

PERSONAL SIDE STORY:

So here's the deal: I used to be all about bread, pizza, and cookies. I mean, who doesn't love a good slice of pizza, right? But then, out of nowhere, I started feeling super sick every time I ate my favorite foods. It was like my body just turned against me. After some tests, the doctor gave me the bad news: Gluten and I were officially breaking up. Yep, I had developed a gluten allergy, and let me tell you, it was not fun.

Suddenly, going out to eat became a whole new challenge. I'd sit there with my friends and family at restaurants, watching them dig into burgers with buns, pasta, and all the things I couldn't have anymore. Meanwhile, I was that person asking the waiter a million questions—"Does this have gluten? Can you make it without the sauce?" Blah-blah-blah… I felt like such a bother, and honestly, it was kind of embarrassing.

And then there were moments when everyone else was enjoying a warm, buttery roll or a slice of cake, and I'd just sit there with my salad or gluten-free whatever, trying not to look too sad. It's not like I wanted to rain on everyone's parade, but sometimes it was hard not to feel a little left out.

But here's the thing, I had to learn to look on the bright side. Yeah, gluten was off the menu, but that didn't mean I couldn't enjoy food anymore. I started exploring all these new gluten-free options and some of them were actually pretty awesome. The amount of things that are commonly gluten-free might surprise you. Almost all types of candy are gluten free! Mind-blowing, right? I had to become a bit of a kitchen ninja, learning how to whip up my own gluten-free versions of my old favorites. It wasn't easy at first, but I figured out how to make it work.

And you know what? I realized that my health was way more important than a slice of pizza. Sure, I still get a little jealous when I see someone else chomping on a donut, but I know that taking care of myself is worth it. Plus, it's kind of cool to be the one introducing my friends to gluten-free goodies they didn't even know existed. And, I'm the cleanest eater out of everybody, and my body totally thanks me for it by staying healthy.

So, yeah, having a gluten allergy isn't exactly a party, but it's taught me a lot about being resilient and finding new ways to enjoy life, even without the bread.

Cool Tips for the Food Sensitive Squad

- **Be a Label Wizard:** Check labels for secret ingredients that might stir up trouble. Talk with your mom or your doctor to find out what to look for to keep you safe.
- **School Lunches:** Pack your lunch when you can, so you know it's safe to eat.
- **Party Planner:** Heading to a friend's party? So fun! Bring a snack you know is safe so you don't miss out on the munching fun. Or, tell your hostess ahead of time what your allergies are. Most of the time, your friends can accommodate your allergy. If you are asked to bring a dish to the party, make sure you bring something tasty that you can enjoy. Then, you can guarantee that you will have at least one yummy thing to eat! It's important not to skip out on the fun.

Eating Well and Feeling Great! 91

- **Educate Your Friends:** Teach your friends about your allergies so they can be allergy-lookout pals.

Having food allergies or restrictions isn't so bad. It makes you unique and teaches you to be careful about what fuels your awesome body. And yes, it's a great excuse to try new, yummy recipes just right for you. So keep rocking that detective hat to make eating safe and fun. High-five to handling your food like a boss!

Knowing When to Eat

It's easy to grab a snack when you're bored or zoning out in front of the TV, but that's a no-go if you want to eat smart. Eat when you're truly hungry, not just because you're bored or because that cookie jar is giving you "the eye." If you're doing something else, like watching a show or scrolling through your phone, try to keep snacks away. This helps you focus on enjoying your food and listening when your body says it's full.

Smart Snacking

Feeling a bit low on energy? Snack time! But choose wisely. Go for stuff like raw veggies, nuts, or low-fat yogurt. Eat snacks that are not only tasty but give you the energy boost you need without the slump from sugary treats.

Best Beverages

Drink up, but make sure it's mostly water. Skip the soda and the fruit punch. Water keeps you hydrated without any extra sugar. It's also great for your skin and overall health.

Take It Slow

Did you know eating slowly can help you feel more full and satisfied with less food? It's true! Or, try using a smaller plate at meals. It tricks your brain into thinking you have more food. Avoid super-sizing when you eat out. Those giant portions are usually way more than one person needs.

Tracking What You Eat

Ever thought about writing down what you eat? Give it a try! When you keep a food diary, you might be surprised by how much (or how little) you're actually eating. It's a cool way to see if you're getting all the nutrients you need.

Everyone is Different

Keep in mind that what works for one person might not work for another. We all need different things from our diets, depending on a bunch of things like how active we are or what our bodies are going through (like a growth spurt).

Need Advice?

As always, if you're not sure about what you should eat, it's a good idea to talk with someone like your parents, a nutritionist, or your doctor. They can help you figure out a perfectly balanced diet and what kind of vitamins would be good for you.

Eating wisely is about making choices that are good for your body and your mind. It's not just about the here and now, it's about setting up healthy habits that will keep you rocking through your teen years and beyond. So, grab that colorful plate, slow down your bites, and enjoy every mouthful. **Your body will thank you for it!**

ACTION TAKEAWAYS:

- Food is your fuel: You need great food during this time of your life.
- Build balanced meals with fruits, vegetables, proteins, grains and dairy in your diet.
- If you have allergies or food restrictions, please don't ignore them when you go out to eat. Tell the servers what you must watch out for and they will tell the chef. When the food is served, look it over and reconfirm verbally that your allergy needs have been met.

14. Sleep: The Importance of Those Zzz's!

Hey, sleepyhead! Ever wonder why your parents are always on your case to get to bed and not stay up late binge-watching your favorite shows? Well, buckle up, because we're floating into the dreamy world of sleep and why it's super important for your mind and your body. Especially when you're growing faster than a YouTube video goes viral!

Why Sleep is Like Your Body's Superpower!

When you're snoozing, your body basically turns into an incredible super-lab—no joke! It's busy fixing muscles, sorting through the day's memories, and recharging your body from becoming a zombie the next day at school.

For all you busy bees buzzing through puberty, getting about **8 to 11 hours of sleep per night** isn't just good, it's a must!

Why so much sleep? Well, your body is like a busy construction site—building muscles, growing taller, and making all kinds of changes, both mentally and physically. That takes a lot of energy, and sleep is when your body recharges its batteries. Plus, your brain is working overtime, too. It helps you remember stuff from school and deal with all those new feelings and experiences.

Think about it: More sleep means you're sharper, happier, and not yawning every two seconds during math class. It also kicks those moody blues away. So yes, catching enough Zzz's makes you a walking, talking ray of sunshine!

Sleep is the Secret Sauce: What's Going On While You're Counting Sheep?

Sleep isn't just for charging up. Nope, it's got a whole menu of benefits. It keeps your heart ticking like a boss, helps you fight off nasty germs, and boosts your brain power. Basically, while you're off in dreamland, your body is in the kitchen whipping up a batch of "stay-awesome" stew!

So, when you're all cozy in bed, drifting off into dreamland, it might seem like nothing is happening, but trust me, your body is busy doing all kinds of cool things while you are sleeping.

First off, your brain is like a super-organized librarian at night, filing away everything you learned during the day. That math formula you struggled with? Your brain is practicing it while you sleep, so it's easier to remember in the morning. It's also cleaning up any mental messes, tossing out the junk you don't need, and making space for new memories.

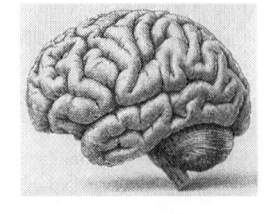

Your body is also in full-on repair mode. If you've got a scrape or a bruise, your cells are hard at work fixing it up while you catch some Zzz's. Muscles recover. Scrapes heal. Cells go to work. Plus, your

Sleep: The Importance of Those Zzz's!

immune system is like a night-shift superhero fighting off any germs trying to crash into your system.

And let's not forget the dream factory! Your brain is cooking up all sorts of wild stories, like you're the star of your own movie. Even weird dreams help process emotions and experiences. So, dreams are actually kind of important.

So, next time you hit the hay, remember that sleep isn't just about resting, it's also when your body and brain do some of their best work!

Here's a Wacky Fact:

While you're asleep, your brain is like a ninja, sneakily moving important stuff from your "recently seen" to your "save forever" memory files. Cool, right?

Why You've Got to Hug That Pillow

Now that you've got the down-low on sleeping, it's time to make your sleep your BFF.

- Set up a cozy bed of comfort with cool pillows and a snuggly blanket or two.
- Get into a chill bedtime routine that tells your body, "Hey, we're slowing down now." Maybe read a book (like this one!), listen to some soothing tunes, or do gentle stretches.

Hitting the sack isn't just something you "have to do," it's your body's favorite time to make everything better. So, wear your pajamas like a superhero costume and dive into bed like it's your secret lair. Tomorrow's adventures depend on tonight's sleep!

Catch those Zzz's, keep munching on good food, and watch yourself transform into the supercharged, mega-awesome YOU!

Nighty-night, *and don't let the bedbugs…* well, you know the drill!

ACTION TAKEAWAYS:

- Sleep is an important time to fix your body and your mind.
- Create a "wind-down" routine to relax your mind and body. This tells your system that it's time to get to sleep.
- You need 8-11 hours of sleep per night.
- Remember: You grow, heal, and get smarter while you sleep!
- Make your bed a cozy space—comfy pillows, blankets, and all.

15. Growing Up: We're Also Talking About Emotions

It's Not Just Physical

Puberty also involves a lot of emotional changes. You might feel more sensitive or get irritated more easily. It's a bummer, but it's a natural reaction to all of these changes. It's all because your brain is developing and your emotions are becoming more complex. You might start thinking about things differently—feeling more grown-up, and in some ways, even start to figure out who you are as a person.

Why Feeling Good on the Inside Matters Just As Much (As Feeling Good on the Outside)

Have you ever noticed how some days you feel great about how you look and who you are, and other days, not so much? It's not just you, everyone has days like that. How we feel on the inside plays a huge part in how we see ourselves on the outside.

What's the connection? Your mind and your body are besties that influence each other big time. Your mental health affects how you feel about your body, and how you feel about your body can impact your mental health. It's like they're best friends who talk all the time. It's hard to believe, but it's 100% true.

Do you want to let your emotions rule you? Probably not, because emotions can be exhausting. So... since your emotions are a choice you can make, you can choose a different emotion (Whaaaat?!).

Seems too simple, right? Well, it is, and it isn't. It takes practice to turn those bad feelings off. But you can't do it until you try, so why not start today? If you're sad, instead of feeling sadness, you can choose to be happy... or grateful... or helpful... or strong... or _____... Fill in the blank, and just be it.

PERSONAL SIDE STORY:

There was this one time at school when I totally bombed a quiz. Like, big time. I felt that familiar wave of frustration and embarrassment creeping in, and I was ready to let it ruin my whole day. But then, something clicked.

Instead of letting those bad vibes take over, I <u>decided</u> to take a deep breath and try something different. I told myself, "Okay, I messed up. But I can either mope about it or use it as a chance to learn." It wasn't easy, but I <u>chose</u> to shake off the negativity and focus on what I could do better next time.

It was kind of like flipping a switch. I realized I didn't have to be stuck feeling crummy. I had the power to decide how I wanted to feel. I could choose to be upset, or I could choose to feel okay and see it as a learning experience. And once <u>I made that choice</u>, everything felt lighter.

Growing Up: We're Also Talking About Emotions 101

So, yeah, emotions can be tricky, but we get to decide how we handle them. Next time something goes wrong, try to <u>flip that switch</u>. You might be surprised how much better you feel!

Mastering Positive Self-Talk

Let's turn your inner voice into your biggest cheerleader!

Have you ever heard that little voice in your head saying you can't do something, or that you don't look good enough? Guess what? You can totally train that voice to be super nice instead! Like, imagine it cheering you on, telling you how awesome you are. It's all about changing the way you think about things and making your inner voice your number-one fan. Let's get those good vibes going!

What is Self-Talk?

Self-talk is basically the things you tell yourself inside your head all day long. It has the ability to shape your self-esteem by bringing it up or bringing it down.

- **Positive Self-Talk:** This is when your voice is all about good things like, "I can totally do this!" and "I look great today!" and "I'm a good friend!"

- **Negative Self-Talk:** This is when your thoughts are being a total downer. Things like: "I'm not good at this," or "I can't wear that," or "No one likes me." Those statements can make you feel horrible, big time. So, let's try some positive self-talk instead.

How to Master Positive Self-Talk

- **Notice the Negatives:** Start noticing when you say mean things to yourself. Catch those negative thoughts and imagine stopping them like a red traffic light. You can literally say "STOP!" or "NO!" inside your head. If you can say no to other parts of your life, you can also say no to negative thoughts.
- **How You Talk to Yourself:** Turn those negatives into positives. Instead of saying, "I'm not good at this," try saying, "I'm getting better every single time I try this."
- **Practice Makes Perfect:** The more you practice positive self-talk, the more natural it will feel. It's like being your own cheerleader.
- **Daily Affirmations:** Every morning, say something nice about yourself. Try standing in front of the mirror and say these nice things to yourself out loud. When you repeat them over and over, they start to stick. Like, "I'm looking great today!" or "I totally rocked that guitar solo!" Write them on sticky notes and put them on your mirror or your laptop. Because when you see them all the time, someday soon, those great thoughts will sink into that awesome head of yours!
- **Talk to Yourself Like You Would a Best Friend:** Think about how you talk to your friends when they feel down. You wouldn't say mean things, right? Talk to yourself the same way that you would talk to your best friends.

REMEMBER:

When you say something, whether it's to a friend or just inside your mind, guess who is the first person to hear it?... YOU. So, make sure your words are kind to yourself and others. It will make your day feel great and you'll be so much happier.

Why Positive Self-Talk Rocks!

- **Positive Self-Talk Boosts Your Confidence Level:** It helps you believe in yourself. Give yourself a good cheerleading session, and you'll feel ready to take on the world!
- **Positive Self-Talk Reduces Stress:** When you're nicer to yourself, you feel less stressed. It's like wrapping your brain in a big, cozy hug.
- **Positive Self-Talk Helps You Do Better:** Believing in yourself helps you do better at school, sports, and in life. It's like your own secret superpower!

<u>Here's a Secret…</u>

Adults use positive self-talk, too! Sometimes, before going into a big meeting where there's a lot at stake, people walk into the bathroom, look in that mirror, and talk themselves up like the superstars they are. Guess what? You can do this, too. The point is, this great pattern of cheering yourself on is something that you can do now, like right this minute. By mastering positive self-talk now, you'll be unstoppable when you're an adult!

The Seven-Day Positivity Challenge!

For the next week, end each day by writing nice things down on paper (not on your phone). Write three positive things you said to yourself that day. Each day, look back on the day before. See how much better you will feel after only one week!

After that, keep that positivity going! The reason we do the seven-day challenge is to let you know how just a small action, like writing positive things down on paper and reading them back, can really make you feel incredible. It can change the way you feel about your life and give you more confidence.

INTERESTING TIDBIT:

Write It Down! Science has proven that writing things down by hand on paper (not on your phone or computer) or in a journal boosts our brain's ability to absorb information. It stays in your memory longer and has a stronger impact on how you feel about yourself. This is a time to set your phone to the side. (Eeeek! I know, but those text messages will still be there when you are finished.)

Your thoughts are powerful, so make them positive. Your inner voice should be your biggest fan, not your biggest critic. Keep practicing, and soon, you'll see how awesome positive self-talk can be. You've got this!

Tips to Boost Your Mental Health and Body Image

- **Healthy Habits:** Positive self-talk, eating well, sleeping, and drinking plenty of water are good for your body. They help keep your mind sharp, too.

- **Stay Active:** Exercise isn't just good for your body; it's also great for your brain. It releases chemicals that make you feel good and happy.
- **Mindful Moments:** Try things like meditation or deep breathing exercises to calm your mind. It's like hitting the pause button on your stress.
- **Positive People:** Surround yourself with friends who build you up and make you feel good about yourself. They're like human sunshine!
- **Talk About It:** Keeping feelings bottled up inside makes them seem bigger. Talk to someone you trust about what's going on in your thoughts. It can really help.

Sometimes, it might feel hard to talk to the people who are closest to you. If that's the case, please ask your parents if a counselor or a therapist is available to you. Any way you can talk about it, please do. It's important to get all your feelings out.

Everyday Strategies

- **Be Kind to Yourself:** Treat yourself as nicely as you would treat your friends. No trash talk allowed.
- **Reduce Screen Time:** Try not to spend too much time on social media can make you feel a little blue. Take breaks and do something fun in real life.
- **Realistic Goals:** Goals that are too big can sometimes seem like too much to tackle, so you might not even try. Break your goals down into smaller steps that feel doable. When they feel doable, guess what? You will actually do them!

- **Gratitude Journal:** Take a moment and write down things you are grateful for each day. It can lift your focus from what you don't like to what you love about your life and yourself.
- **Take Action:** Actually go out and do the things you are thinking about and writing in your journal. Sometimes emotional stress comes from lack of action. So, get off the fence and just do it!

Today is Only One Day, Tomorrow Will Be Better!

Hey, even if today totally stunk, guess what? Tomorrow is a brand new day full of new opportunities!

If things didn't go your way today, maybe you bombed a quiz, or had a fall-out with a friend. Don't sweat it! Tomorrow is a fresh start where anything can happen. It's all about keeping that hope alive.

Knowing that tomorrow is there is like knowing you have a reset button in the game of life. Super powerful!

Try to think about the cool stuff that can happen next in your life, like acing that test you studied for, or making up with your buddy, or getting the lead in the play you auditioned for, or even someday inventing the cure for cancer! Hey, it could happen!

So, toss today's stress in the trash and get pumped for a better tomorrow. Every new day is a chance to make something awesome happen!

Growing Up Takes Time

You might be super fast on the track team, but when it comes to growing up, you've got to slow that vibe down. Be patient. To feel good about yourself, it's important to take care of your mental and physical health. When your mental health is in a good place, it's easier to see yourself in a positive light. Feeling good mentally also gives you the energy to chase your dreams and enjoy life.

As you go through the intricate maze of all these changes, it's really important to have people you can talk to—like your parents, older siblings, or teachers. They can help you understand what's happening and give you support when you need it.

So, take a deep breath... in... out... in... out...

The thrilling journey of becoming your true self is just the beginning. So exciting, right?! I'm thrilled for you and your future!

Always remember that it's okay to ask questions and talk about your feelings. You're not alone. Everyone goes through this growing up thing, and there are a lot of people who can help you along the way. Rock On!

ACTION TAKEAWAYS:

- Practice positive self-talk every day.
- Look in the mirror and say nice things out loud to yourself.
- Whenever you think or say something, you are the first person to hear it. Make those thoughts positive and kind!
- Write positive things down on a piece of paper or in a journal. You will remember them better.
- Flip the switch! Decide to be happy and find a better way to deal with your emotions. If something goes wrong, change the script by turning your negative feelings into a positive reaction.
- You can get out of your negative funk by just deciding to be positive. It's that easy!
- Be kind to yourself. You are a work in progress.
- Growing up takes time.
- Please share with your parents or a trusted adult if you're having a rough time. It's important to include them in the

good times, also. Emotions can sometimes be exhausting, and sharing them with your parents or a trusted adult can be incredibly helpful.

16. Exercise: Move Your Way to Happy!

Let's get moving! Not because you *have to* or because you're trying to look a certain way, but because it's fun, and it feels good. It's also a great way to keep those positive mental vibes going. Let's find ways to get active in a way that makes you smile, helps you chill out, and keeps you healthy for all the adventures you've got ahead. Exercise rocks!

And read this chapter to the end…

Because I'm going to share an exercise adventure that I did (and maybe you can also do someday) that is low-key, **AMAZING!**

Why We Exercise

It Makes You Feel Happy!

Ever notice how you feel totally amped and happy vibes after a hard-core sports game or jogging? Have you ever heard of a "runner's high"? That's because exercising is like a secret weapon for boosting your mood.

When you get moving, your body releases these amazing chemicals in your brain called *endorphins*. They are like nature's happiness ingredient and make you feel super good. One of the best ways to get endorphins is to work out. It can't get much easier than that!

Endorphins hit your bloodstream when you score a winning goal, run a hard race, or nail a tough game. You normally feel it just after, and it feels like you can conquer the world! It's pure awesome! The cool thing is, now that you know the science behind it, when it happens to you, you'll be like, "Hey! Those are those endorphin things, and wow, they feel great!"

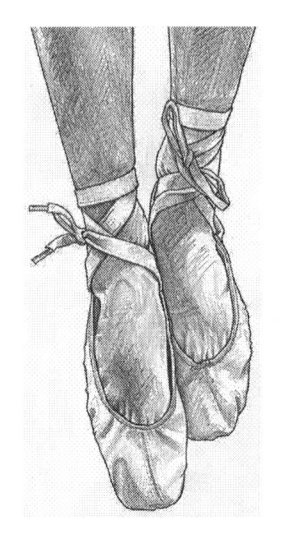

Exercise a Stress Zapper

Burning off some energy can help get rid of stress and chill out those grumpy vibes. If you find yourself feeling down or kind of *blah*, just grab your gear and get active. It's a sure-fire way to flip your mood from "meh" to "Yeah!"

Energy Burst

Here's the deal: Exercise isn't just about getting fit. It's also like a super-charged energy drink for your body, but way healthier! When you get up and move, whether it's shooting basketball hoops, doing some yoga, or just a quick jog, it seriously wakes up your whole body. It's kind of like when your phone is low on battery and you plug it in—Bam!—it's ready to go again!

Exercise keeps your blood pumping and oxygen flowing. It makes you feel more awake and ready to tackle anything from homework to hanging out with friends.

If you're sleepy or sluggish, just a bit of exercise can boost your energy levels, big time. Trust me, it's like hitting the refresh button on your day!

Heart Health

Your heart is like the boss of your body's action center, and keeping it happy is super important. Exercise isn't just for adults or pro athletes. It's key for your age, too, and it keeps our hearts healthy.

When you're sprinting in soccer, dancing ballet, or even just skateboarding, your heart starts pumping and grows stronger with each beat. Think of your heart as a muscle that gets more powerful the more you work it out. This means it can pump blood around your body easier, which keeps you feeling energized and ready to tackle anything.

Staying active sets you up for a healthy heart later on in life. That way, you can keep doing all your favorite things for years and years to come.

So, grab your sneakers and let's keep our hearts in tip-top shape! Moving around pumps up your heart rate, which keeps the heart muscle strong and healthy. This means you can run, jump, and play sports without running out of breath so quickly.

Making Exercise Part of Your Life

- **Set Realistic Goals:** You don't have to run a marathon or climb a mountain right away. Maybe start with something easy, like walking your dog every day after school or doing 10 minutes of yoga in the morning. The important thing is just getting started, and keeping it going.

- **Mix It Up:** It's important to have variety because different exercises use different muscles. It also makes it way more fun! So, mix it up! Try different activities to see what you enjoy the most. Maybe you'll find out that you love something you never thought you would.
- **Involve Your Friends:** Sometimes having a buddy can make exercising a lot more fun. Challenge a friend to a bike race or join a team. You're more likely to stick with it if you're having fun with friends.

Finding Fun Ways to Stay Active

- **Play Sports:** Whether it's kicking a soccer ball, swinging a tennis racket, or shooting hoops, competing in sports is a great way to stay active. Plus, you get to hang out with friends and maybe even be part of a team.
- **Dance It Out:** Put on your favorite tunes and dance around your room or take some dance classes. Yoga, salsa, hip-hop, cardio dance, ballet, tap, jazz—there are a lot to choose from! It doesn't matter if you're making perfect moves. What matters is you're moving and having fun.
- **Adventure Outdoors:** Go for a hike, ride a bike, or get a friend and walk through your neighborhood. It's a great way to explore new places and see the cool things around you, all while getting some good exercise.

Think Outside the Box

One of my favorite things to do is go mountain biking! YES!! Did you know that was a thing? Riding your bike on a dirt path on the side of a mountain is pure awesome! It's an incredible way to see the outdoors, and when I'm doing it, it feels like I'm flying!

Do an internet search on different types of exercise. There are so many ways to work out your body!

And Hey, Think Big!

Don't think of exercise as only being in your "backyard". You can also think big. Maybe talk to your parents about organizing a future adventure trip to:

- Hike a famous mountain with your family.
- Explore a National Park.
- Walk a famous trail that your ancestors traveled.
- Go to a summer adventure camp.
- Bike in another state or country.
- Try adventures around the world!

These types of adventures take time and sometimes money, but WOW! Am I right?!

YOU'LL NEVER BELIEVE THIS!

Someday, when you're older, you could even go to another country and swim in the deep blue ocean with humpback whales like I did! Talk about endorphins! WOW! (Hey, did I just low-key, **BLOW YOUR MIND?!!!**) Just think about how amazing it would be to swim right next to a giant mama whale and her newborn baby. I'm here to tell you—it's absolutely incredible!

You can't do any of these things without a great heart and continued exercise! And guess what? It's fun!

Start Small and Then Think Big, Superstar!

Who knows, with great exercise throughout your life, you could become a famous pro athlete, a high-profile surfer, or a world adventure photographer! No matter what path you choose for your future, famous or not famous, exercise is still the closest thing to magic you can give your body. So, pull out your magic exercise wand and do your best "Abracadabra!" And after you've nailed that exercise, give your body a big "Tah-dah!" Because you did it for YOU!

ACTION TAKEAWAYS:

- Exercise: 1. For feeling happy. 2. For an energy burst. 3. For heart health. 4. To get rid of stress. 5. For adventure!
- Think big! Think about the future.

17. Let's Compare... Let's Not!

Social Media—Keeping It Cool and Positive

Have you ever seen those amazing pictures online in magazines or on social media and wondered why everyone looks so perfect? Well, it's time to let you in on a secret—there's a lot of digital magic going on.

SIDE NOTE:

We're going to touch on social media here. However, we do a deep dive on how to handle all of that (and more) in the ***MY SOCIAL POWER!*** book, so make sure you pick up a copy of that. It's really important stuff. What you see here is just a sneak peek!

Almost Everything You See is FAKE

Comparing yourself to others online is like watching someone's highlight reel and thinking it's their everyday life. But what you see isn't always what's real!

What's Up with the Media?

The media—like TV shows, movies, magazine ads, and social media—often show us pictures and videos that have been changed to look more beautiful or impressive. Here's what's really going on.

- **Photoshop:** It can make people look thinner, remove zits, and even change eye color! There's almost nothing that Photoshop cannot change.
- **Filter Frenzy:** Filters are like magic wands that make a very regular photo look like a fashion shoot.
- **Perfect Poses:** Notice how models always seem to have the best pose? That's no accident. They're told how to stand or sit to get the perfect shot.
- **Lighting Tricks:** Lighting can totally change how something looks in photos. Bright lights can make flaws disappear, and shadows can add muscles where there aren't any.
- **Artificial Intelligence:** Yeah, and artificial intelligence (AI) can literally pull pictures out of thin air. It's impossible to compete with that.

How to Be a Media Detective

- **Question It:** See a picture that looks too perfect? Ask yourself, "What have they changed in this picture?"
- **Reality Check:** Compare what you see in the media to people around you. Notice any differences? That's because real life isn't Photoshop!

- **Learn the Lingo:** Understand terms like "airbrush," "edited," and "filter." Knowing what they mean helps you spot when they're being used.
- **Awareness:** Talk about media tricks with your friends and family. Spread the word that what we see isn't always real life.

Why Comparing is Not So Great

When we see perfect pictures and compare ourselves, it's impossible to live up to something that has been digitally changed. If you were to see some of these people in real life, you would be shocked. They are just regular people like you and me. Yes, some of them have a certain beauty that they are born with, but they don't look anything like they look in their *Photoshopped* or filtered pictures.

Some of your friends might even be editing their own pictures with apps on their phones. I mean, have you noticed how some of them never look as good in real life as some of the pictures they put on their feed? That's because a lot of it is fake.

Often, we compare our normal self to someone else's best fake moments. This can make us feel like we're not good enough, and that feels pretty crummy.

Don't get caught up in the trickery, my friend! You're so much better than that fake stuff.

Missing Out on Stuff

When you spend so much time comparing yourself to others, you miss out on the cool stuff you're doing yourself. It's like being so busy taking videos at a concert that you forget to enjoy the music.

What is Your Goal on Social Media?

Are you...

- Wanting to share what's going on in your life?
- Wanting to keep a diary of your adventures?
- Wondering about other people's lives?
- Searching for new things to learn?

OR

- Are you searching for "Likes" and hearts?

Hmmmmm... if it's the last one, then we've got a little work to do. Let's look into reframing our view of how social media can help us and not hurt us.

Looking at Social Media Another Way

Another way to look at your social media feed is to think of it as a history book about you. If you look at it from the viewpoint, "Hey, I just love putting my life down on the screen." Then it's not about getting likes FOR THE QUALITY of your life. This is you trying to KEEP A RECORD of your life, and other people get a chance to look at it.

If you look at it from that viewpoint, you have kept your power. Once you start searching and hoping for "likes," you're giving up your power to people who might not care about you; who might even try to hurt you. There are people out there who enjoy being mean. They are called mean girls, bullies, and haters. You cannot control people's responses, and some of these kinds of comments can be very hurtful and damaging.

Let's Compare... Let's Not!

You keep your power by FOCUSING ON YOUR ACTIONS instead of wishing for people's good comments or "likes." When you focus on the cool things you are DOING and NOT focus on how they are responding, then they lose that power over you.

You matter a lot—way more than any online drama. Your mental health and safety are what's really important. Try to stop focusing on that online fake world and focus on you in your real world. Your real world is much more interesting!

A Game Plan to Avoid Comparing

- **Focus On You:** Instead of looking at what everyone else is doing, focus on your own goals and what makes you happy.
- **Keep a Journal** or a list of things you're proud you achieved, even the small wins.
- **Take Screenshots of Fantastic Emails or Texts:** Put them all in a folder labeled "My Great Messages!" That way, when you're feeling a little down, you can look up those great moments, and they will help get you back on track!
- **Celebrate Your Unique Self:** There's only one you, and that's your superpower. Embrace your good things, your quirks, and all the things that make you different. They are what make you interesting!
- **Limit Social Media Scrolling:** Social media can make it super easy to fall into that comparison trap. Maybe spend a little less time scrolling. But when you do, remind yourself that you're seeing their best bits, not their everyday lives.

Turning Comparisons Into Positive Goals

If you admire someone else, instead of trying to be exactly like them, change it to how you can achieve something similar. For example, if you think someone is fantastic at sports and you want to be too, don't aim to be like them overnight. Start small, like practicing your skills or trying out for a local team.

- **Get Inspired, Not Discouraged**: Let other people's successes inspire you instead of getting you down.
- **Talk About It:** If you're feeling down about comparing yourself or you don't know how to stop comparing, talk to someone about how you're feeling. They might help you see all the great things about you that you're overlooking.

BONUS PRO TIP:

Guess what? The most amazing girl in the room isn't the one who looks like she just stepped out of a magazine. Nope. The most amazing girl is the one who rocks her self-confidence like a total boss. She's the one who totally stands out just by being herself. And guess what? That girl can be you!

It all starts with having a super positive attitude. Try to see yourself as the awesome person you are. Let your amazing qualities shine brightly. Focus on all the best parts about you, and forget about digging in that negativity drawer for anything else. Stop doubting yourself, okay? Be proud of yourself for giving it your all. And trust me, when you feel great about who you are, it totally shows!

QUOTE:

"I believe in being strong when everything seems to be going wrong. I believe that happy girls are the prettiest girls. I believe that tomorrow is another day, and I believe in miracles."

— Audrey Hepburn

Everyone moves at their own pace. Comparing yourself to others is like trying to play a sport without enjoying the game—it takes all the fun out of it. Focus on your own game, enjoy winning your own personal goals, and remember that you're doing great just as you are.

… and **SMILE**!

Keep rocking what you've got! Use other people's good points to help you move forward, but don't use them as a measuring stick.

ACTION TAKEAWAYS:

- A lot of what you see is FAKE.
- Don't miss out by only focusing on "likes" and hearts.
- Screenshot great texts and emails that make you smile.
- Use positive self-talk.
- Try to limit social media.
- Look around you for inspiration.
- Focus on the great things you are doing.
- Smile! "Happy girls are the prettiest girls…"

18. Support Crew: Creating Your Own Circle of Awesome

Have you ever felt like you're all alone? You're not, but I know it can feel that way sometimes.

Everyone needs someone, and most of us need a group of "someones" to help us deal with what life throws at us. I'm talking about the kind of people who lift you up and cheer you on. Building a solid support community can make a huge difference in how you see yourself, how others see you, and how you face the world. Let's find out about building a helpful support network that keeps you strong and confident.

Everyone Has Strengths and Weaknesses—Pluses (+) and Minuses (-)

Nobody is 100% perfect. Whether we know it or not, we often reach out to other people to help us fix things that are broken or missing in our lives. These people can help us fix our weaknesses, and fill in some of our minuses (-).

Why Is a Support Community So Important?

When you're part of a supportive group, everybody in that group helps each other. Imagine being part of a super squad where everyone shares their superpowers! Just like "The Avengers," your support team works together to make a better world. You can create your own *"Avengers"* team that works together to make you a better person! And guess what? You, with all your strengths, help them to become better people, too. It's like being on a dream team where each person has their own special moves to help the group win.

A great support system is like working together as a group to create better versions of each other! By you bringing all your great stuff and them bringing all their great stuff, you create an unstoppable force that helps you through even the most difficult challenges. Hello, Avengers!

Glimpse Into Adulthood:

There's an old business phrase that might help you understand this concept of support community.

"What do you bring to the table?"

In companies all over the world, people often gather around conference tables for business meetings. Each person brings something different and important to the group's goal.

1. One person might be super creative: meaning they know how to "create" the goal.
2. One person might be great at strategy: meaning they know how to "accomplish" the goal.

3. One person might be great at marketing: meaning they know how to "sell" the goal.
4. One person might be great at art: meaning they know how to "visually demonstrate" the goal.
5. One person might be good at safety: meaning they know how to "safely build" the goal.
6. One person might be great with money: meaning they know how to "pay" for the goal.

Do you see where I'm going here? Everybody "brings something to the table," (adds something valuable). The same thing happens in your support crew. Everybody "brings something to the table"—you included!

Here's the question…

What Do *YOU* Bring to the Table?

What are you bringing to your group? Whatever the answer to that question is, it's important because you're an important part of your support crew. Without you, the group wouldn't have this great insider knowledge on _____ (fill in the blank).

And, without them, you wouldn't have whatever _____ they bring to the table:

Maybe your super strength is:

- Humor
- Compassion
- Soccer skills
- Math skills
- Help with _____
- Being the cheerleader
- The list is endless!

Everybody brings something special, and most of the time, each person is great at more than one thing.

Sometimes, it's hard to figure out what those awesome things are that you bring to the table (that value you add). But know that even if you can't figure it out, <u>you do bring some awesome, undefinable things</u> to your friendship table. You are important to the group, and people within the group are important to you.

You can also find something new to bring to the table! Brainstorm about something new you'd like to learn, something you'd like to share. Then research it, learn it, and OWN IT! It's all in your power!

You—yes, YOU—are essential! It's like a magical soup of awesome that is hard to put into words but somehow **works to create a more fantastic you, a more fantastic them, a more fantastic group, and a more fantastic life!**

The Value of a Group that Supports You

- **They Give Advice and Cheer You On:** Got a problem? Your supportive community offers advice based on the life problems they've had or the victories they've made. It's like having someone there, writing a personal guidebook just for you.
- **Feeling Like "I Belong!":** Knowing you're not alone with your problems and feelings can make all the difference. A great support group helps you handle almost any problem you have in this ever-changing and growing thing we call life.

Support Crew: Creating Your Own Circle of Awesome

How to Build Your Community

- **Join Clubs or Groups:** Look for clubs at school or in your community that match your interests. It's a great way to meet people who like the same things you do.
- **Volunteer:** Helping in your community can connect you with others who want to make a difference. Plus, it feels good to do good!
- **Be Open and Kind:** Sometimes, being friendly can open doors to new friendships and connections.
- **Use Social Media Wisely:** Get interested in groups and pages that focus on positivity and body confidence. Join in conversations that make you feel good about yourself.

Tips for Growing Your Community

- **Be a Good Listener:** Sometimes, just being a good listener can be the best way to help support somebody.
- **Share Your Story:** Being open about your experiences helps others to share, too. This can deepen the connections within a group and build trust.
- **Celebrate Each Other:** Cheer your friends on when they succeed and lift them up when they're down. Celebrating small wins and helping each other through tough times can strengthen your friendship and build trust.
- **Stay Positive:** Try to keep conversations uplifting and encouraging. A positive vibe can be contagious!

Why Community Matters

Your support community is like your team in the game of life. They celebrate with you, catch you when you fall, and help you grow into your best self. Together, you can face anything that comes your way with courage and confidence.

Building your community takes time, but every friend you make, every group you join, and every positive interaction you have adds to that supportive circle that surrounds you with love and positivity.

Are you feeling inspired yet? Think about it this way—every kind action you take helps make the world brighter for everyone. You're going to make the world shine!

ACTION TAKEAWAYS:

- You need people, and people need you. Together, you make a great support crew.
- What are the things you "bring to the table"? Everybody brings something special to the group (adds something valuable).
- Got questions? Ask someone you trust. Support is part of your power!

19. Role Models: Finding Your Squad of Superstars!

Have you ever seen someone do something so awesome that it made you want to jump in and try it, too? That's the power of having a role model!

Role models can be like real-life superheroes who show us that anything is possible, no matter what. Not only do they show us what is possible, they also teach us how to make the impossible happen. This chapter is about finding those people who inspire you to be your best self and chase your dreams!

Why Role Models Rock!

Role models are super important because they show us the ropes, inspire us to overcome challenges, and teach us it's cool to be ourselves.

Here's What Makes Role Models So Great:

- **Lead By Example:** Seeing someone achieve their goals can motivate you to achieve your own.
- **They Show Us What's Possible:** If they can do it, why can't you? Role models help you see the potential in yourself.
- **They Teach Us How to Bounce Back from Obstacles:** Learning about their struggles and how they overcome them can give you strength during your tough times.
- **They Sometimes Show Us How to Avoid the "Hard Way":** If someone could show you a smarter way to do something, wouldn't you want to try it? Role models can teach us how to avoid "bumping our noses" (making common mistakes) by showing us the BEST way to do something. They've already figured out the pitfalls. It's like having a cheat code for life! They can teach us how to do things smarter, not harder.
- **You Can Find Role Models Online:** You see a superstar online? Sure, you can follow them, but follow wisely…

IMPORTANT INSIGHT:

Personally, I sort of have a problem with the modern usage of the word *"follower"* in social media. It supports that mean kid/bully social structure that makes it seem like some people are better than you (FALSE!). It's just that right now, at this moment, those people you're considering on social media might just be more popular than you, more famous, or have an interesting skill.

HOWEVER, someday YOU also might have all of those cool attributes, including an interesting skill that you just haven't discovered yet. AND, you could become famous for something, we just don't know yet! Your life has only just begun!

Role Models: Finding Your Squad of Superstars!

Seeing the word *"follower"* everywhere makes the word so common in your vocabulary that **you might think that your role in life is to follow everybody. When, in fact, your important role in life could be to LEAD**! So, NO! *Following* is not your role.

Let's make a campaign to live in the world of being a "Leader" more often instead of being a *follower*.

When you click the *"follow"* button on a site, I would love for you to have this mental note instead: I want you to think "I'm *Interested*" *instead* of thinking "I'm *following*." Let's be *interested* in something or someone instead of just *following*. Being interested is active participation, while *following* is just being a passive sponge.

I know, you're probably thinking, *"Follower*. It's only a *word...*" Yeah, you're right, but **words matter.** How do you feel when someone compliments you? Great, right? Well, those are just words... And when someone insults you? Pretty crummy, right?

All of those are just words... But all of those words have power over you. Do you see where I'm going here? **WORDS MATTER.**

How to Find Your Role Models

- **Look Around:** Your role model could be anywhere—maybe a teacher, a coach, an older sibling, or even your friend.
- **Read Up:** Books and documentaries about people who have done amazing things can be very inspiring.
- **"Get Interested" (Follow) Wisely:** Find people on social media who share positive messages and show real glimpses into their lives.
- **Think Close, Think Far:** Your role model doesn't have to be famous or so distant from you. They can be someone in your community, in your neighborhood, or even in your home. It

could even be your Mom and Dad. They just need to be someone who makes you want to be better.

Tanya's Story

"There's this person in my life who's, like, my absolute role model—my big sister, Mia. She's five years older than me, which makes her seem grown-up and wise. But the coolest thing about Mia is that she's always been there for me, no matter what.

"Mia's got this way of making everything seem like it's going to be okay, even when I'm freaking out. Like, this one time, I had the biggest pimple ever right on the tip of my nose, and I was seriously considering skipping school because of it. But Mia just looked at me and said, 'You know what? Pimples are like badges of honor. They mean you're growing up, and that's really cool.' Then she handed me her favorite concealer and showed me how to cover it up like a pro.

"She's also the queen of confidence. Mia is always reminding me to love myself just the way I am, which isn't always easy when you're my age and everyone seems to have their lives together on social media. But she's always telling me that 'those pictures aren't real, those are just their happy times. No one ever posts their sad times. No one posts their troubles, and nobody's perfect 24/7.' One time, she even posted a selfie with no make-up, bedhead, and a big zit on her forehead, just to prove a point. It was hilarious (and so brave!)

"Mia is also super smart and works really hard in school, but she never makes me feel dumb if I don't get something right away. Instead, she'll sit with me and explain things until I get it. She says, 'There's no rush. Everyone learns at their own pace.' And that's something I really admire about her. She's so patient, so kind, so helpful, and she believes in me.

"So yeah, Mia is my hero. She's funny, smart, and totally confident in herself. She makes me want to be like her someday."

That's Tanya's story. You might notice that she didn't have to look very far in the universe to find her role model. You can do the same thing. Or maybe you have a dream about becoming a pro athlete and joining the Women's Basketball Association (WBA), or some other grand design for your life. You can DM them (direct message). You can contact famous people through social media, and sometimes they might even reply. I know for a fact that many pro athletes do respond to some messages and give helpful hints on how to do things.

IMPORTANT PRO TIP:

Make sure the role model you are looking at is worthy of your attention.

You need to analyze each role model and make sure that they are a truly positive person and can teach you something good. Just because someone is famous or flashy doesn't mean they're worth copying. Some people who look like good role models might actually have their own hidden agenda.

Why Finding Good and Trustworthy Role Models Matter

Good role models can help guide you through life's ups and downs. They can help you see the beauty of your journey, even when things get tough. They can teach you the best (and sometimes easiest) way to do something. By following in their footsteps, you learn to carve your path and grow into the great person you're meant to be.

Tips to Be Inspired Every Day

- **Set Goals Like Your Role Models:** Look at what they have achieved. Set similar goals for yourself, whether it's being kinder, nailing a project, or learning a new skill.
- **Ask Questions:** If you can, talk to your role models or direct message (DM) them. Ask for advice on how they treat certain situations.
- **Stay Curious:** Always be on the lookout for new people to admire and learn from. Inspiration can come from the most unexpected places.
- **Be a Role Model Yourself:** Remember, you can also be someone else's role model! Start by being the person you'd look up to.

Be the Role Model Everyone Looks Up To

Have you ever looked at someone and thought, "Wow, they are so cool. I want to be just like them"? Guess what? You can be that person for someone else. Yep, you've got the power to inspire, lead, and make people go, "Whoa, they've got it together." And the best part? Being a role model isn't about being perfect (because nobody is). It's about showing up, being kind, and standing tall—even when things are tough. Let's talk about how you can be the ultimate role model for others.

How to Be a Role Model for Other People

Being a role model isn't about having a magic wand or being a super-hero (unless you're into capes—then go for it!). It's about setting a good example with your actions, words, and choices. Here's how:

Role Models: Finding Your Squad of Superstars! 135

- **Be kind:** Yeah, just be kind. It's so easy! Hold the door, compliment someone's new haircut, or just smile at people. Kindness is free, and it makes you shine like a star.
- **Stay true to your values:** If you believe in something, stick to it. Being honest, working hard, and treating people with respect will send a clear message: These acts show the world what matters most to you.
- **Admit when you mess up:** Being a role model doesn't mean you do everything right. You might mess up sometimes, because we're all human. If you make a mistake, own it and apologize. People will respect you even more for it.

Role models don't just talk the talk, they *walk the walk*. When others see you doing the right thing, they want to follow your lead.

What Does *"Walk the Walk"* Really Mean (And Why It Matters)?

It means that if I suggest that you do something, then I am going to be doing it too. No exceptions. I'm not just going to let you be out there dangling by yourself—No, I'm going to be doing the exact same thing, setting the example of how to do it, and then actually doing it right alongside you.

Using Your Voice to Stand Up for What's Right

Sometimes, being a role model means speaking up even when it's hard. It could be standing up for a friend, calling out unfairness, or simply saying, "Hey, that's not cool." Your voice is powerful, so don't be afraid to use it! Here's how:

- **Practice courage in small ways:** Start by speaking up in low pressure situations, like suggesting a group activity or politely disagreeing with a friend. It will build your confidence for bigger moments.
- **Stick to facts, not drama:** If you're calling out bad behavior, stay calm and focus on what's wrong. For example, "It's not fair to leave people out," works way better than shouting, "You're being a jerk!"
- **Have your squad's back:** If you see someone being treated unfairly, don't stay silent. A simple, "Hey, that's not okay," can make a huge difference. (Make sure it's safe to do this. If not, please go get an adult to help.)

Using your voice shows others that doing the right thing is worth it. It also inspires them to find their own courage. That's a total role model move!

IMPORTANT:

Please make sure that the situation you are in is a safe situation in which to call people out. If you are in a set of circumstances where you notice things are getting out of hand, getting physical or somewhat dangerous, it's important to find an adult and get them involved. Please don't take on dangerous situations by yourself.

Inspiring Confidence in Your Friends and Peers

Here's a secret: Confidence is contagious. When you believe in yourself, it rubs off on the people around you. And when you hype up your friends, you're like a walking pep squad. Here's how to be a confidence booster:

- **Be their cheerleader:** Celebrate your friends' wins, big or small. Did they ace a test? "You're a genius!" Nailed the

Role Models: Finding Your Squad of Superstars!

soccer goal? "Whoa! You're giving me MVP vibes!" Your support can turn a small win into a huge confidence boost!
- **Remind them of their strengths:** When a friend says, "Ugh, I'm so bad at this," hit them with a list of all the things they're amazing at. Confidence level => Boosted.
- **Demonstrate by being brave first:** If your group is nervous about something (like joining a new club), be the first to try it out. Your bravery will inspire them to follow your lead.

When you lift others up, they'll start believing in themselves as well. And guess what? That makes *you* feel more confident, too. It's a win-win!

You're Already a Rockstar

Being a role model doesn't mean being perfect or having all the answers. It's about showing kindness, standing up for what's right, and helping others see their own strengths and potential. Isn't it incredible that you can have that impact on another person?

You've already got what it takes to inspire the people around you. So, go out there, be your amazing self, and let your actions shine like a warm sun of positivity. The world needs more role models, just like you!

Everyone has someone they look up to. Finding your own role models is like choosing the best coaches for TEAM YOU. They cheer you on. They show you the way. They push you to rise above your challenges, and they help inspire you to reach every star you dream of grabbing!

ACTION TAKEAWAYS:

- Role models are important in our growth and social development. They inspire us, teach us, and help us become better people.
- Talk to your parents about your role models. Let them help you analyze if they are someone worthy of your attention.
- Sometimes, you don't have to look far to find a fantastic role model. They might just be in the next room cooking dinner, doing homework, or watching TV.
- You can be a role model, too! Don't be shy, let that sunlight shine!
- If you have any questions, please talk it out with your parents, siblings, or teachers.

20. Fashion and Expression

Dress to Express, Not to Impress!

Have you ever put on an outfit and felt like you could conquer the world? Or maybe you tried something on and it just "didn't feel like *you*?" That's because clothes are more than just what we wear—they are a way to express who we are! Let's find out about using fashion to show off your cool style and boost your confidence, all while staying true to yourself.

Why Fashion Matters

Fashion is a great way to show who you are without having to say a word. Here's why it's kind of amazing:

- **Self-Expression:** It shows off your great personality. Are you a sports fanatic? An art guru? A fashion trendsetter? Show it off!

- **Boosts Your Mood:** When you're dressing in the morning and checking yourself out in the mirror—all those colors, and patterns, and great style will make you smile ear to ear. It's like a little blast of happiness every time you look in the mirror.
- **Creativity:** Changing up your outfits lets you feel creative. Think of your wardrobe as your own personal paint canvas!

How to Rock Your Style

- **Wear What You Love:** Don't worry about what everyone else thinks. If you love what you're wearing, your confidence will shine brightly. When you're in your favorite clothes, you might even start a trend!
- **Experiment:** Try different styles and see what feels best. Borrow clothes from friends or family to mix things up without spending money.
- **Choose Comfort:** Choose clothes that fit great. Comfort is the key to feeling good!
- **Accessories:** Hats, scarves, jewelry, and even purses add a fun twist to any outfit. They're like the cherry on top of a fantastic chocolate sundae!
- **Colors and Patterns:** Bright colors can be super energizing, and cool patterns can turn a plain outfit into something special.

Dressing Your Best Feels Great

Choosing your own style helps you feel more independent and confident. It's not about dressing to impress others, it's about feeling good about yourself and owning your look. When you feel good on the outside, it matches how you feel on the inside, too.

Grab your gear, and start expressing yourself through your fashion. Every single day is a chance to show the world a little more about who you are!

So get out there and glam it up! Show the world your style!

ACTION TAKEAWAYS:

- Fashion has a big way of helping you boost your confidence.
- Use patterns, stripes, polka-dots, pictures of bunny toes, whatever! Just show off your style!
- Shop your own closet or trade with friends.
- Go shopping for fun things that you feel good in and fit your style.

21. Embracing Your Unique Sparkle

Let's talk about something super cool: Diversity! Now, I know it's a big word, but it's actually all about what makes each of us special in our own way. Let's look at how amazing it is to be different and why it's worth celebrating!

What Does Diversity Look Like?

First things first, diversity means that people come in all shapes, sizes, colors, and personalities—like a giant collection of awesomeness! Think about your friends: Some might have curly hair, some might have straight; some might be tall, others short; some might love math, and others are all about art. Diversity is what makes the world interesting and colorful. Imagine if everyone looked the same, acted the same, or liked the same things. Boring, right? It's our differences that make life fun!

Why Should We Celebrate Our Differences?

Okay, so now that we know what diversity is, let's talk about why it's so cool. When we celebrate our differences, we're basically saying, "Hey, you're awesome just the way you are!" It's like making someone feel great about their uniqueness. This not only makes others feel good, but it also helps you appreciate your own special qualities.

Celebrating differences teaches us to be open-minded and kind. It helps us understand that everyone has their own story and experiences. Plus, when we learn from others who are different from us, we become smarter, kinder, and much more interesting.

PERSONAL SIDE STORY:

Growing up, everyone around me was pretty much the same—same clothes, same music, same everything. It wasn't weird, it's just what I knew. It's just how life was, and frankly, I didn't know that there was something else out there. (You don't know what you don't know, until you know, you know?!)

When I moved to the big city, it was like stepping into a whole new world. Sure, I met a lot of different people in my youth, but my real exposure to diversity came when I moved to a different state.

My first week, I met people from places I'd only seen on maps. A new friend was from a country I couldn't even spell (Sri Lanka), and a girl in ballet could speak three languages like it was no big deal. At first, I felt like a total fish out of water because I didn't know how to connect with people who were so different from me.

But as I got to know them, I realized our differences weren't something to freak out about or get in the way. Our differences were actually pretty awesome. My new friend from Sri Lanka introduced me to foods that I had never even heard of, and my ballet friend taught me some cool phrases in different languages. We started sharing stories about our lives, and it hit me: Our differences made us way more interesting.

One day, I was sitting in my room thinking back about fun memories. I was thinking about all the fun things I did with these new and creative people in my life. I realized that, even though we came from totally different backgrounds, we had so much in common. We all had crushes on people, wanted to do fun things, and we all wanted to make the world a better place.

Learning to embrace diversity didn't happen overnight. It took time to get used to, but as I opened up to new cultures, ideas, and people, my world got so colorful. I didn't just learn to accept diversity, I really loved it. It showed me how our differences make the world more interesting and that when we come together, we can do amazing things.

How Can You Celebrate Diversity?

You don't have to wait until you move to a different state like I did. You can start NOW, and it's easier than you think! Here are some great ways:

- **Get to Know Different Cultures:** Try learning about the foods, traditions, and holidays of different places around the world. You could even try cooking a new recipe with your family or watching a movie from another country.
- **Be Friends With People Who are Different From You:** Don't just stick with people who are exactly like you. Mix things up! Make friends with people who have different interests, backgrounds, or styles. Diversity enriches our lives.
- **Compliment Others on Their Unique Traits:** See something cool about someone else? Tell them. Maybe it's their epic

curly hair, artistic eye makeup, or their great sense of humor. Just make sure that it's a genuine compliment, and not just something you want to throw out to everyone. If you compliment everybody, then the power of your compliments weakens. It will seem like, "Oh, she says compliments to everybody—don't get too excited." You don't want that to happen, because when you compliment someone, it can really be powerful, and you want it to be a big deal for them. So make sure it's sincere, and then spread the love.

- **Celebrate Your Own Uniqueness:** Love what makes you, YOU. Maybe you have a unique talent, like drawing, or maybe you love to read about space. Whatever it is, embrace it and don't be afraid to share it with the world.

How Can You Make Others Feel Good About Being Different?

Now, let's talk about being a superhero in real life by helping others feel confident about their own uniqueness. Here are some cool ways to do that:

- **Stand Up for Others:** If you see someone being teased because they're different, stand up for them (if it's safe. If not, get an adult). Let them know they're awesome just the way they are. Your support can make a huge difference.
- **Include Everyone:** When you're hanging out with friends, make sure no one feels left out. Invite everyone to join in, even if they're a little different.
- **Be Kind:** Sometimes, a simple smile or a kind word can make someone feel great about themselves. Being kind costs nothing, but it's worth everything.
- **Encourage Others to Be Themselves:** If you notice someone hiding what makes them special and unique, encourage them

to let it shine. Whether it's their love for a certain hobby or their cool fashion sense, let them know it's okay to be themselves.

The Bottom Line

In the end, being confident in your own body and personality is all about loving what makes you unique and appreciating the diversity around you.

Now, go out there and explore the people and things that differ from you. Celebrate yourself, celebrate others, and remember that the world is a much better place because of all of our differences. You'll learn a lot about other people and cultures when you do this, and you might just learn a little something about yourself, too.

So, go out there and spread some positive vibes! Let's cheer for every difference, because diversity is not just beautiful, it's powerful!

ACTION TAKEAWAYS:

- Some forms of diversity are our body shapes, skin colors, and hair types, to name a few.
- Celebrate what makes you, YOU, and what makes them, THEM.
- Celebrate the different types of people in the world. We are all part of a giant garden of differences.
- Compliment people, but make sure it is sincere. It will make you both feel great inside!
- If you are curious about where you are from, ask your parents or a trusted adult to find out the answers to these questions. It will probably be a great conversation!

22. Kindness is Your Superpower!

Are you ready to level up on your social confidence? Being confident isn't just about rocking your own vibe, it's also the fact that when you give back to others, you're empowering your soul! Whoa! Total power move!

Being Kind is the Ultimate Tool

Being kind is like having your very own superpower. It's not just awesome for the people you're kind to, it's amazing for you, too! Every time you share, lend a hand, or dish out a compliment, it sprinkles a little happiness into your day as well as theirs. Imagine this: Every act of kindness is like giving your heart a big snuggle-hug. Feeling good yet?

HERE'S A HUGE INSIGHT

This is one of the most important things in this book...

People—ALL PEOPLE—just want to feel love.

EVERYONE.

Everyone includes you... me... teachers... policemen... the gal that charged you for those jeans you just bought... even mean girls... everyone.

Simple, right? Seems so obvious. Like, really? But, yes, it's true. And, sadly, that one simple thing is so often ignored.

That one simple thing—making someone else feel noticed and loved—will pretty much define your personal and emotional success in this world.

And, this pursuit of feeling this love and sending out the feeling of love to others will be a lifelong process.

AND IT WILL BE POWERFUL!

And do you know why it will be powerful? Because it is sincere, because it comes from your heart connecting with someone else's heart, and that's magic in its most powerful form—heart-to-heart connection!

This *love* can come in many different ways:

- Emotional connection
- Physical action, like a hug
- Attention
- Respect
- Admiration
- The list goes on...

So, what's the secret? You just need to find a person's *currency*.

What is Currency?

Okay, so here's the deal: Everyone has their own thing that makes them light up like a Christmas tree plugged into an extra long extension cord. It's called their *"currency."* And no, I don't mean money (but yeah, I'll take my allowance early, thank you!)

Currency is like the emotional food they need to live.

For some people, it's as simple as sharing a snack—like, you offer them a brownie, and suddenly, you're their new BFF! Other people? Compliments. Tell them their hair is giving out "all-star vibes," and they'll be smiling for a week. Others? Maybe it's respect… or attention, or…

The trick is finding out their *thing*. Like, if your friend is obsessed with their pet hamster (seriously, why does it have its own Instagram account?!), ask them about it. Watch how fast they go from "meh" to "let me tell you EVERYTHING about Mr. Peanut the Third."

But hey, here's the best (and sometimes the hardest) part: Finding someone's currency is like going on a treasure hunt, but instead of gold coins, you get people who suddenly want to sit with you at lunch. Sometimes, finding that thing that "lights them up" and smile from ear to ear is not easy to do. But, when you do find that *thing*, they will perk up like a neon sign! Because, they will think:

This person actually *SEES* me. They *GET* me.

After that, they will actually listen, and they will want to be heard, and all this will happen in a very positive way. So, get out there and crack their code!

The Great Feeling of Helping Out

Got some time? Share it! Helping others isn't just nice, it's powerful. Whether you're handing out food at a shelter, hanging out with someone who needs a friend, or tidying up your local park, you're doing big stuff. These things connect us to others and show how small acts of kindness can make a huge difference.

Charity: Your Time to Shine

Think about what you're good at. Maybe you're a math genius or a sketch artist. Why not share those skills? Tutor someone, lead a craft day, or share whatever makes you light up. Charity is not only about giving money, giving your time and talents are also great ways to give back to the world.

How to Make Others Feel Included and Valued

When you're the kind of person who makes everyone feel like they belong, you're like the VIP of kindness. It's really not that hard. Got a new kid at school? Invite them to sit with you at lunch. Notice someone left out of a group or game? Scoot on over and say, *"Hey, come join us!"*—Boom!—instant hero move.

Making people feel included is like being the captain of your own kindness ship, steering towards sunshine wherever you go. You're sailing through the high seas of negativity, and picking up those passengers who might feel lonely or awkward. And trust me, when you do this, you're not just being kind—you're being a superhero. So, grab your imaginary captain's hat, and start by making waves of kindness.

How Small Acts of Kindness Make a Big Difference

Here's the thing: Kindness doesn't have to be a big, sparkly, fireworks moment to count. It's actually the little stuff that makes a huge difference. Smiling at someone in the hallway? Yep, that could totally turn their crummy day around. Saying "good job" when your friend crushes a math quiz? Yes again! It's like giving their brain a happy dance.

Every nice thing creates a "ripple." That ripple can reach further than you think. Everything nice you do, no matter how small, creates a tiny "splash" in the universe. And the ripples from that splash have the strength to radiate from person to person. You might not see it, but your kindness could inspire someone else to be kind, and then that could inspire someone else to be kind, and—okay, you get the point. Basically, your kindness is like a secret chain reaction of awesomeness. High five, kindness Ninja!

PERSONAL SIDE STORY:

I was at the grocery store pushing my cart down the aisles and picking up my favorite snacks. As I reached the checkout line, I noticed a lady in front of me with a worried look on her face. She was counting her money and putting back some of her items because she didn't have enough money to pay for everything.

Feeling a tug at my heart, I leaned forward and said, "Excuse me, but I'd like to take care of your groceries today." The lady looked at me with wide eyes and tears starting to form. "Are you sure?" she asked, her voice shaking. "Absolutely," I replied with a smile.

As she left the store, she waved goodbye and had a big smile on her face. I felt a warm glow in my heart. It felt amazing to give back and to help someone else in need. Small acts of kindness can make a big difference in someone else's day.

Work It at School

Why not kick off a kindness club, lead a good deed challenge, or start a smile-spreading mission at school? Showing others how fun and rewarding it is to help out can really fire up a positive chain reaction. It's a great way to spread smiles and good energy all around.

Every time you lend a hand or flash a smile, you're not only brightening someone else's day, but you're boosting your own, too. So, go on, spread some good deeds around, and watch your confidence climb as you see the impact you make. Let's bring our superpower of kindness into the spotlight and change the world bit by bit.

Ready to Be a Kindness Hero? It All Starts by Saying YES!

ACTION TAKEAWAYS:

- Kindness is your superpower!
- You will feel great when you help others.
- Giving to others isn't only about giving money, your time and your skills are just as important.
- When people see you doing good deeds, it makes them want to do good deeds, as well.
- Got questions about how you can make the world a better place? Talk it out with your parents or a trusted adult.

23. Most Important Chapter in this Book, and I'm Not Kidding!

Superhero Action—All Month Long, All Year Long, All Life Long!

Hey you, Superstar! Can you believe we're already at the end of the book? Congratulate yourself on your own personal growth!

I know we've been focusing a ton on what happens during puberty and being on your period. Some of it takes getting used to, but here's the scoop—the rest of the month is just as important for keeping your vibe high and yourself feeling awesome, for like, forever!

Let's break down why taking care of yourself and believing in yourself is your secret sauce to rocking your BODY POWER all month long, all year long, all life long.

Who Do You Want To Be When You Grow Older?

Treat yourself and reach for those wild dreams! Go on, you can do it! I'd love to hear all about your success stories!

I ask this now, not because you need to know exactly *WHAT* you want to be when you grow older, but it is important to start figuring out *WHO* you want to be and create that positive mental attitude.

You may not know it, but your adult life has now begun!

Congratulations and Welcome to the Big Show!

Belief in yourself and your skills is a huge part of getting where you want to be in life. What a great time to learn this! While you're adapting yourself to understanding your body, you might as well apply these same ideas and turn them into some great life skills.

This May Be the Most Important Part of this Book (And I'm Not Kidding!)

Hidden within these chapters, where I've been writing (and joking around) about dealing with puberty, mastering your mood swings, and taking care of and loving your body—these are literally the same skills you need to master the skill of life!! (Whaaat?!) Yeah, that's right!

You have all the basic tools in your toolbox now, so rework some of these sentences, wiggle the word "body" out of "My Body Power!" and guess what you're left with … **"MY POWER!"**

That's right! Say it out loud! "MY POWER!!" Scream it, if you want! "MY POWER!!"

Most Important Chapter in this Book, and I'm Not Kidding!

Hahahaha!! I love it! Because, you know what? You can own this, this power of yours. And trust me, I'm not joking with you—when you believe it and you live it, YOU LITERALLY ARE POWERFUL!

So say, "Take that, you crummy puberty-dog, you period-monster! You're not going to get the best of me! I've got MY POWER! I've got all these great tools to slay you and any other fire-breathing dragon that comes along my path!"

Because Going Through Puberty…

- Is making me stronger!
- Is making me wiser!
- Is making me take care of myself!
- Is making me understand that all the strength that lies within me is only just starting to wake up!

Exciting, isn't it?

Who knew that going through puberty was going to be so outrageously important?

Every woman who has walked before you has gone through puberty, but not every woman has understood her power.

I think I should repeat that, because it is so important!—**not every woman has understood her power.**

Please take this beautiful change in your life, and instead of just getting through it, instead of letting it rule you, take your amazing power and own it! Go forth and conquer, warrior queen!

IMPORTANT: Yes, all of these ideas are great, but you have to apply them to your life to make them work.

I repeat, **YOU HAVE TO APPLY THESE IDEAS TO YOUR LIFE TO MAKE THEM WORK!**

Now Let's Switch Our Talk to YOU Owning All of This Incredible Knowledge!

I NOW KNOW HOW TO:

1. Love my own unique body!
2. Keep track of my water intake!
3. Enjoy a healthy diet!
4. Value my routine!
5. Handle my period!
6. Take care of my grooming!
7. Keep an eye on my sleep needs!
8. Decide if shaving is right for me!
9. Appreciate my curves!
10. Appreciate my friends!
11. Journal my thoughts!
12. Keep my attitude positive!
13. Educate others!
14. Bring something to the table!
15. Be a support to others!
16. Create my own support team!
17. Listen to my body!
18. Deal with my emotions!
19. Say NO to things that aren't right for me!
20. Seek out reliable advice!
21. Think and talk about myself in a positive way!
22. Know that I'm not alone!
23. Tomorrow is another day!
24. Practice smart and safe social media rules!
25. Have good people that I look up to!
26. Cut myself some slack!
27. Don't compare myself to pics I see in magazines or online!
28. NEVER give out my location or sensitive information to people online!

Most Important Chapter in this Book, and I'm Not Kidding!

29. Make good choices. Everything in life is choices!
30. Know that kindness is my superpower!
31. Celebrate our differences!
32. Find great and honorable role models that are worthy of my attention!
33. Be a leader, not a follower!
34. Surround myself with a wonderful support crew!
35. Find clothes that make my new shape look great and make me smile!
36. Talk with my parents or a trusted adult to find the answers to my questions, or to vent my feelings!
37. Know the power and structure of setting goals!
38. Learn how to "sell myself," so that my super talents, skills and personality will shine!
39. And… **FEEL MY POWER!**

My puberty is just the first step in this beautiful dream we call life. And I understand that what was once "My Body Power!" is now actually me claiming my strength, my body, **_"MY POWER!"_**

💜 💜 💜

Thank you for letting **_MY BODY POWER!_** be a part of this journey with you! I hope you found this book helpful.

Help someone else find the help they need! And you can be the reason for their success!

★ ★ ★ ★ ★ RATE

1. **Click the Link or Scan the QR Code**!

https://dub.sh/ALLA

2. **Share your feelings:** How did it help you? Did it make you smile? Did you have an "Oh, I get it now!" moment?

3. **Please leave a GREAT STARS ★★★★★ WRITTEN REVIEW** letting everyone know what you loved about the book, so other people will get the help they need also!

4. **Maybe add a picture or video** of yourself along with your review and online talking about how the book helped you! I'd love to see who you are! #MyBodyPower!

Want more tools for your confidence journey? Check out these other empowering reads:

- *MY SOCIAL POWER!* (For Boy & Girl Tweens, Teens and Young Adults)
- *MY PERIOD POWER!* (For Girl Tweens, Teens and Young Adults)
- *MY SOCIAL POWER! WORKBOOK* (For Boy & Girl Tweens, Teens and Young Adults)
- *MY PERIOD POWER! WORKBOOK* (For Girl Tweens, Teens and Young Adults)

Now go out and grab your POWER!

Acknowledgements

Writing **MY BODY POWER!** has been such an incredible experience, and it would not have been possible without the love and support of so many amazing people who helped me along the way.

First and foremost, a huge thank you to YOU—the reader! Whether you're just starting out on your journey with body confidence or you've been building body confidence for a while, I'm so proud of you for picking up this book. I wrote it with you in mind, and I hope it gives you the tools you need to feel strong, empowered, and confident in your own skin. I'm so excited to be a part of your journey!

A big thank you to my incredible family, who have always encouraged me to be bold and go after my dreams. You've given me the confidence to pursue projects like this one, and your endless love and support mean the world to me. To my incredible family—especially my parents—for always encouraging me to dream big and never give up on my big dreams. You taught me the importance of self-love and confidence, and that has shaped everything I have done in my life and have written.

I also want to express my deepest gratitude to Dr. Renee Cotter, who graciously wrote the foreword for **MY BODY POWER!** Your expertise, wisdom, and passion for helping young people embrace their bodies have had a huge impact on me and this book. While you didn't write this book, your support and guidance have been invaluable, and I'm so thankful to have your voice included.

To all the health professionals, educators, and body positivity advocates out there—thank you for the important work you do every day.

Your efforts to empower young people to love themselves and to take care of their bodies inspire me, and this book wouldn't be what it is without the important work you've contributed to this field.

Lastly, a massive shout-out to my talented publishing team who brought **MY BODY POWER!** to life. Every detail of this book has your magic touch, and I'm so grateful for your dedication and hard work in making this project shine.

To every young person reading this—thank you for being brave, curious, and open to learning more about your body. I hope this book helps you embrace the changes, challenges, and joys that come with growing up.

A Special Note to You, the Reader…

You are powerful and wonderful, just as you are, and I believe in you every step of the way.

With love and gratitude,

SheriBelle Karper

About the Author

SheriBelle Karper is a true citizen of the world, uniquely equipped to share wisdom on confidence and self-empowerment. For years, she's been an adventure photographer, traveling across the globe (often solo), seeking out new faces, wild places, and unforgettable experiences. She has set foot in a jaw-dropping number of countries. That kind of globetrotting takes some serious confidence.

Through all her travels, SheriBelle has had a front-row seat to some of life's most extraordinary moments. She's danced with tribes in Africa, petted wild Icelandic ponies, and whacked her way through the dense jungles of northern Thailand while trekking alongside elephants. She stood among the solemn bomb sites of Sarajevo, witnessing history's lingering scars, and watched families in Nepal say sacred goodbyes during beautiful afterlife ceremonies. From joy to loss, from wilderness to wonder—she's seen it all.

One of her most unforgettable moments? When she traveled solo to the country of Tonga to freedive in the vast Tongan Trench! (It is the second-deepest ocean trench on Earth, plunging more than an astonishing 35,000 feet. Although, she didn't freedive that far down!) Swimming in those wild, rolling waters—only a few yards from massive humpback whale mothers and their newborn calves—she captured the magic through her professional underwater camera lens. SheriBelle recalls locking eyes with one mother whale, describing it like this: "It felt like I was right there with something god-like, something beyond words, something immensely powerful—like whatever created the sun and the moon… That kind of power? That kind of connection? That kind of adventure? Yep, that takes confidence!

In 2018, when Hawaii's Big Island was first rocked by a volcanic eruption, SheriBelle Karper was right there, capturing history in real time. She spent five intense days behind the lines with the National Guard, shooting alongside media giants like CNN, Fox News, and NBC. Only a few crews were allowed to go back each day, and SheriBelle was among them. Wearing a hardhat, goggles, and a gas mask, she listened as the National Guard's monitors beeped louder and faster—warning of deadly gases in the air. At one point, the wind shifted. She and the team had to sprint to safety, their vans screeching away, just in time. She even took three daring open-door helicopter flights to photograph the lava spewing beneath her. Sitting up front with the pilot, leaning halfway out of the chopper with her camera in hand, SheriBelle captured the breathtaking chaos of that erupting volcano. Fearless confidence, indeed!

But SheriBelle's boldness isn't confined to her global adventures. She's also a multi-award-winning and nominated screenwriter and author, celebrated for her comedic wit and sharp storytelling. She's even taken the mic at Los Angeles's legendary comedy club, *The Improv*, performing stand-up for live audiences. Stand-up comedy? That's another arena where confidence is a must!

Her social impact extends beyond the wild and the far away. At home, SheriBelle has spent years empowering young people. She served on the board of a major charity supporting at-risk youth, spearheaded a graffiti-removal program in partnership with a major paint company, and even trained in grief counseling for high school students because she believes so deeply in helping teens navigate life's tough moments.

She's been acknowledged by Los Angeles City and County leaders for her dedication to creating opportunities for teens. She's even enjoyed many years of volunteering at her kids' schools, where she's seen firsthand how confidence and curiosity go hand-in-hand.

And while all of SheriBelle's adventures are extraordinary, her greatest and most fulfilling experience has been raising her two children—her ultimate source of pride. In her words, "They are beautiful and gifted in each their own way, and live fearlessly, with humor and honor." While raising them, SheriBelle has practiced everything she shares in her books, proof that confidence begins at home.

SheriBelle has had all these extraordinary life experiences: From photographing the world's wildest corners to free-diving with whales, to cracking jokes on world-famous stages, to winning awards for her writing, to raising two amazing kids, to fleeing a violent volcano, just to name a few. And somehow, still made it back in time for school pickup. All of these experiences have shaped SheriBelle Karper into a woman who knows what it takes to face life's challenges head-on. She knows that she can trust herself and move through the world with strength and courage. Now, she's bringing that same bold spirit to her writing, crafting confidence guides like ***MY SOCIAL POWER!, MY BODY POWER!, MY PERIOD POWER!, MY SOCIAL POWER! WORKBOOK,*** and ***MY PERIOD POWER! WORKBOOK,*** to help young people discover their own inner power and confidence during this very important time of their lives.

Whether she's swimming with humpbacks, writing award-winning stories, or helping teens embrace their unique journeys, SheriBelle

Karper is on a mission to inspire confidence in all its forms, and she's here to help *you* find yours!

Now it's your turn! What will your adventure be? What kind of confidence are you ready to grow? Whether it's making a new friend, trying something new, or speaking up for what matters to you. This is your moment. Let's go!

Other Titles by SheriBelle Karper

— — **YOUNG ADULT** — —

The MY POWER! Series
https://Dub.sh/MyPowerSeries

MY PERIOD POWER! (Period Confidence Guide: For Girls - Tweens, Teens and Young Adults) ★★★★★
https://Dub.sh/MyPeriodPowerBook

Also Available In Spanish. Soon in French, German, Italian, European Portuguese, Brazilian Portuguese, Japanese, Simplified Chinese, and Russian

MY SOCIAL POWER! (Social Confidence Guide: For Boys & Girls - Tweens, Teens and Young Adults) ★★★★★
https://Dub.sh/MySocialPowerBook

Also Available In Spanish. Soon in French, German, Italian, European Portuguese, Brazilian Portuguese, Japanese, Simplified Chinese, and Russian

---

MY PERIOD POWER! WORKBOOK (Period Confidence Workbook: For Girls - Tweens, Teens and Young Adults) ★★★★★

Also Available In Spanish. Soon in French, German, Italian, European Portuguese, Brazilian Portuguese, Japanese, Simplified Chinese, and Russian

---

MY SOCIAL POWER! WORKBOOK (Social Confidence Workbook: For Boys & Girls - Tweens, Teens and Young Adults) ★★★★★

Also Available In Spanish. Soon in French, German, Italian, European Portuguese, Brazilian Portuguese, Japanese, Simplified Chinese, and Russian

♥

— —MEMOIR— —

WHY THE WIDOW WEARS BLACK ★★★★★

♥

Other Titles by SheriBelle Karper 169

Please check out all the other titles at
KingmanPublications.com

Kingman Publications LLC

Glossary and Words to Know

Acetaminophen: It's a kind of medicine. You can take it when you have a headache or cramps during your period. It helps make the pain chill out. Just make sure that you **talk to your parents and your doctor** before taking any medication.

Acne: When your skin gets all bumpy and red because of too much oil and dirt clogging your pores. It's like your skin's way of saying it needs a good wash!

Amenorrhea: This is when someone doesn't get their period for a while. It's not about having it once and then skipping; it's more like never starting or taking a very long break. It could be because of stress, diet, or too much exercise.

Areolae: The dark circles around your nipples, kind of like a bull's-eye on a target—it's where babies feed.

Birth Control: These are the ways to prevent pregnancy when you're older and decide to be close with someone. There are lots of types, like pills, or special devices a doctor can help with. This book doesn't go into detail about this, but it is a very important subject to talk with your parents and doctor about.

Blackheads: Dark spots on your skin, especially your nose and forehead, where oil and dirt have gotten stuck and turned dark.

Bloating: Ever feel like your belly is all puffy and full of air? That's bloating. It can happen before or during your period, and makes your clothes feel tighter.

Breast Bud: The early bump under your nipple that shows your breasts are starting to grow. It's the first step in growing breasts!

Caffeine: A zippy ingredient in coffee and soda that can keep you awake and bouncing off the walls if you have too much. It isn't good to have it too late in the day. Rest is very important during your period.

Calcium: A super important mineral for your bones, making them strong and tough. It gives you a strong skeleton.

Clitoris: A tiny, sensitive spot at the top of your vulva.

Consent: A big deal word that means saying yes or no to things that affect your body. It's about making sure everyone's cool with what's happening.

Cramps: Ouch! These are the achy pains in your lower belly you get when your period shows up. It's like your body's way of telling you it's cleaning house.

Cycle Tracking: Keeping an eye on when your period comes and goes, so you can guess when it'll visit next. Helps you not get surprised by your period's "hello."

Dandruff: Annoying white flakes in your hair, coming from your scalp. It's like your head's way of saying it needs some extra tender, loving care (TLC!)

Delayed Puberty: When your body takes a bit longer to start the growing and changing phase.

Dermatologist: A doctor who knows all about skin and helps you when you have pimples, rashes, or other skin stuff going on.

Glossary and Words to Know

Discharge: A whitish fluid that comes out of your vagina. It is totally natural and part of your body keeping itself clean.

Dysmenorrhea: A fancy word for super painful periods. Like, when the cramps are so bad, you just want to curl up and not move.

Endometrium: It's the inside layer of your uterus, where the period blood comes from. Every month, it gets ready for a baby, and if there's no baby, it breaks down and comes out as your period.

Estrogen: One of the body's hormones that helps girls become women, especially during puberty. It also plays a big part in the menstrual cycle.

Fallopian Tubes: The twisty pathways in your body, where eggs travel from your ovaries to your womb, like nature's little conveyor belts.

Fertility: It's about whether you can make a baby. When you're older, fertility means your body is ready to get pregnant if you decide to have kids.

FSH: This stands for Follicle Stimulating Hormone. It's a hormone that tells your ovaries to get an egg ready each month for your period cycle.

Genitals: Your private parts down there, including your vulva, vagina, and everything inside and out that's involved in the reproductive system.

Growing Pains: The aches and pains you feel in your body, especially legs, as you stretch and grow taller during growth spurts.

Growth Spurt: When you suddenly grow a lot taller in a short time, like you're shooting up faster than a weed in the garden.

Gynecologist: The doctor that you go to for female health and related problems. They are your go-to source for all period matters. Plus, you will continue to see your gynecologist throughout your adult feminine life.

Hormones: These are like your body's messengers. They tell different parts of your body what to do, like when to grow, or when it's time for your period.

Hygiene: This is about keeping clean, especially during your period. It means changing pads or tampons regularly and washing up to feel and smell fresh.

Insomnia: When sleep plays hard to get, and you just can't fall asleep, or stay asleep, no matter how tired you are.

Intercourse: A grown-up thing where two people's bodies come together in a special, intimate way, often relating to making babies.

Ibuprofen: A medicine that helps with pain and swelling. Great for tackling those period cramps or when you've got a headache. Make sure you talk to your parents and doctor before taking any medication.

Labia: The two sets of lips around your vaginal opening, part of the vulva, that protect and cover your inner private parts.

LH Surge: This stands for Luteinizing Hormone Surge. It's a big hormone wave that tells an egg to leave the ovary. It's a key part of the menstrual cycle.

Meditation: Chilling out on purpose. Sitting quietly and letting your mind take a break from all the noise and busyness.

Menarche: Fancy term for your first ever period. It's a big step in becoming a teenager and means your body is doing its thing.

Menopause: Way later in life, when a woman's period says "bye-bye" for good, and she stops being able to have babies.

Menstrual Cup: A reusable cup you can use instead of pads or tampons. It catches your period blood and is eco-friendly because you wash and reuse it.

BONUS: When you are ready to check out menstrual cups, take a look

Glossary and Words to Know 175

at the end of this Glossary where you will find a chapter about period cups.

Menstrual Cycle: The whole process your body goes through to get ready for a possible baby each month, ending with your period if there's no baby.

Menstrual Equity: This is about making sure everyone who gets their period has what they need, like pads or tampons, no matter their money situation.

Menstrual Hygiene: All about taking care of yourself during your period using period products the right way and keeping clean to stay comfy and healthy.

Menstrual Phase: This part of your menstrual cycle is when you actually have your period. It's the body's way of getting rid of the inner lining of the uterus when there's no baby.

Menstrual Products: These are items like pads, tampons, and menstrual cups that you use to manage your period. They help collect the blood so you can go about your day.

Menstruation: Also means having your period. It's when blood and tissue from your uterus come out through your vagina. It's a normal part of being a girl and happens once a month.

Mood Swings: When your feelings change super fast, like being happy one minute and sad the next. It can happen around your period because of hormone changes.

Nipples: The pointy bit on your breast where milk comes out if you ever have a baby. They can be sensitive to the touch.

NSAIDs: Stands for nonsteroidal anti-inflammatory drugs. These are medicines like ibuprofen that help with pain and swelling. Good for dealing with cramps. Make sure you **talk to your doctor and parents** prior to taking any medication.

Ova: A fancy word for eggs, the ones in your ovaries, not the fridge! They're part of what can make a baby when the time is right.

Ovaries: These are two small organs that hold all your eggs. They also make hormones like estrogen and progesterone, which help control your period.

Ovulation: This is part of your menstrual cycle, when an ovary releases an egg. It's the time when you can get pregnant if you're older and having sexual intercourse.

Pads: Pads are like soft, absorbent stickers you put in your underwear to catch blood. They come in different sizes for light or heavy days. (See also: Tampons, Menstrual Cup, Period Underwear.)

Peer Pressure: When friends or classmates try to nudge you into doing something you're not so sure about. It's like the pushy friend that tries to convince you to do something that you may not want to do. It is very important to talk to your parents, or a trusted adult, if someone is pressuring you to do something you don't feel is right for you.

Pelvic Inflammatory Disease (PID): This is an infection in the female reproductive organs. It's not about having your periods; these can be caused by STDs (Sexually Transmitted Diseases). It's important to know about for your health.

Period: Another word for menstruation. It's the few days each month when blood comes out of your vagina, a sign that your body is working right. It's totally a normal part of growing up—a powerful sign that your body is working!

Period Poverty: This is when girls and women can't afford period products, which makes it hard for them to go to school or work during their period.

Period Stigma: This is a weird or negative attitude some people have about periods. It's not cool, because menstruation is natural and happens to half of the population.

Glossary and Words to Know

Period Tracking: Your "*My Period Power! Workbook*," and other tools like this that can help you keep track of your menstrual cycle. It can help you predict when your period will start and help you notice any patterns or changes.

Period Underwear: Special underwear that has extra layers to absorb your period blood. You can wear them instead of, or as backup to, pads or tampons.

Polycystic Ovary Syndrome (PCOS): A health condition where women have higher levels of certain hormones, which can make periods irregular and cause other symptoms like hair growth and acne.

PMS (Pre-Menstrual Syndrome): The physical and emotional symptoms that some girls and women get before their period starts, like cramps, mood swings, and bloating.

Precocious Puberty: When puberty shows up super early, like a guest arriving way before the party starts.

Progesterone: A hormone your body makes that helps control your menstrual cycle and gets your uterus ready for a possible pregnancy each month.

Puberty: The big change-o-rama—when your body goes from kid to teen, getting ready for all the grown-up stuff, like growing hair in new places, getting taller, and starting your periods.

Reproductive Health: This is all about the health of your reproductive system. It includes periods, but also things like going to the gynecologist and making sure everything is working right.

Sanitary Napkins: Another name for pads. They're used to absorb blood and keep you feeling clean and dry.

Sexual Health: This is about taking care of your reproductive system and making safe choices about sex. It includes using protection and getting checked for sexually transmitted diseases and infections.

Sexual Intercourse: When two adults get really close and connect their bodies in a way they show love or make babies. It's part of grown-up relationships. It's always okay to say "No."

Spotting: This is light bleeding that can happen between periods, or when you're not expecting your period. It's usually nothing to worry about, but can be a sign to check in with a doctor if it keeps happening.

Sustainable Menstruation: Using products like menstrual cups, reusable pads, or period underwear to help the environment. It's all about having a period without creating a lot of trash.

Tampons: A product you insert into your vagina to absorb blood. They come in different sizes for different flow levels and are invisible from the outside.

Toxic Shock Syndrome (TSS): A rare, but **very serious** illness that can happen if you leave a tampon in for too long. It's why it's important to change them regularly. **SIX HOURS MAX** to help avoid this rare but important risk!

Urethral Opening/Urethra: The tiny hole where your pee comes out: Right below your clitoris, not involved in menstruation, but super important for going to the bathroom.

Uterus: Your baby house! It's the special organ where a baby can grow if you decide to have one later. Each month, it preps for a possible baby but sheds its lining as your period if there is no baby.

Vagina: The stretchy tunnel that connects your outside parts to your uterus, where your period blood comes out, and where babies are born from.

Vulva: The whole outer area of your female private parts, including the labia, clitoris, and the openings to your vagina and urethra.

Resources & References

Here are some great articles that I enjoyed reading and got a lot of information from. They could be great resources for YOU!

Take your time and read through them to see which ones might answer your questions.

♥

7 Amazing Facts about Periods that Everyone Needs to Know – Helping Women period. (2019, April 9). https://www.helpingwomenperiod.org/7-amazing-facts-about-periods-that-everyone-needs-to-know/

10 Strategies for Boosting Self-Esteem in Teen Girls: for teachers. (n.d.). https://www.fearlesslygirl.com/blog/10-strategies-for-boosting-self-esteem-in-teen-girls-a-guide-for-teachers

11 Signs your Period is Coming: Symptoms & How to Tell. (2024, September 24). Natural Cycles. https://www.naturalcycles.com/cyclematters/signs-your-period-is-coming

Acne (for teens). (n.d.). https://kidshealth.org/en/teens/acne.html

All about periods (for teens). (n.d.). https://kidshealth.org/en/teens/menstruation.html

All about puberty (for kids). (n.d.). https://kidshealth.org/en/kids/puberty.html

Atif, H., Peck, L., Connolly, M., Endres, K., Musser, L., Shalaby, M., Lehman, M., & Olympia, R. P. (2022). The impact of role models, mentors, and heroes on academic and social outcomes in adolescents. *Cureus*. https://doi.org/10.7759/cureus.27349

Ayon. (2023, April 28). *The 5 surprising benefits of helping others teens need to know*. HRF. https://www.harrisonriedelfoundation.com/the-5-surprising-benefits-of-helping-others-teens-need-to-know/

Barendse, M. E. A., Cheng, T. W., & Pfeifer, J. H. (2020). Your brain on puberty. *Frontiers for Young Minds*, *8*. https://doi.org/10.3389/frym.2020.00053

BBC - Science & Nature - Human Body and Mind - Teenagers. (n.d.). https://www.bbc.co.uk/science/humanbody/body/articles/lifecycle/teenagers/growth.shtml

Blessing, & Blessing. (2020, July 24). *How would you describe or sell yourself? | Lluvia Health*. Lluvia Health - Child and Adolescent Health NGO Nigeria |. https://www.lluviahealth.org/how-would-you-describe-or-sell-yourself/

Boys & Girls Clubs of America. (2024, June 5). *The Importance of Goal-Setting for Teens - Boys & Girls Clubs of America*. https://www.bgca.org/news-stories/2022/January/the-importance-of-goal-setting-for-teens/

Brauner, A. M. (2001, August 22). *Period problems: What they mean and when to see the doctor*. WebMD. https://www.webmd.com/women/features/period-problems-what-they-mean-when-to-see-doctor

Brazier, Y. (2023, April 21). *What to know about puberty*. https://www.medicalnewstoday.com/articles/156451

Bruce, D. F., PhD. (2023, February 10). *Teens and acne.* WebMD. https://www.webmd.com/skin-problems-and-treatments/acne/what-is-acne

Bryant, C. W. (2023, March 8). *Top 10 things you should not share on social networks.* HowStuffWorks. https://computer.howstuffworks.com/internet/social-networking/information/10-things-you-should-not-share-on-social-networks.htm

CHOC. (2023, June 23). *Social Media Tips for Kids and Teens - CHOC - Children's health hub.* CHOC - Children's Health Hub. https://health.choc.org/handout/social-media-tips-for-kids-and-teens/

De Jong Md PhD and Shashwati Pradhan, J., MD. (n.d.). *Getting your period: What is a 'normal' menstrual cycle for teens and preteens?* UChicago Medicine. https://www.uchicagomedicine.org/forefront/pediatrics-articles/getting-your-period-normal-menstrual-cycle-teens-preteen

Department of Health & Human Services. (n.d.). *Puberty.* Better Health Channel. https://www.betterhealth.vic.gov.au/health/healthyliving/puberty

Discover the Joy of Moving & Getting Fitter! - Unbeaten Fitness Richland. https://unbeatenfitnessrichland.com/discover-the-joy-of-moving-getting-fitter/

Dove. (n.d.). *The Dove Self-Esteem Project | DOVe.* https://www.dove.com/us/en/dove-self-esteem-project.html?gad_source=1&gbraid=0AAAAADiRVcKsFetkxyFRBX1V7fn0OzrDF&gclid=EAIaIQobChMIodnrpqabiQMVUxitBh0LByFUEAAYASAAEgKu5_D_BwE&gclsrc=aw.ds

Fleming, W. (2024, February 7). *How to help your daughter deal with a mean girl friendship.* parentingteensandtweens.com. https://parentingteensandtweens.com/help-teen-daughter-manage-mean-girl-friendship/

Fletcher, J. (2023, April 25). *What to eat on your period to relieve symptoms*. https://www.medicalnewstoday.com/articles/what-to-eat-on-your-period

Fremont, E. (2024, October 15). *Which role models will benefit your teens most?* Center for Parent and Teen Communication. https://parentandteen.com/character-role-models/

Garey, J. (2024, August 16). *10 tips for Parenting Preteens*. Child Mind Institute. https://childmind.org/article/10-tips-for-parenting-your-pre-teen/

Girl to Woman: Your Changing Body during Puberty. (n.d.). WebMD. https://www.webmd.com/teens/ss/slideshow-girls-changing-body

Gongala, S. (2024, September 18). *Mean girls at School: types, characters and how to deal with them*. MomJunction. https://www.momjunction.com/articles/how-to-deal-with-mean-girls-at-school_00398481/

Growth and normal puberty. (1998, August 1). PubMed. https://pubmed.ncbi.nlm.nih.gov/9685454/

Healthdirect Australia. (n.d.). *Puberty for girls*. Physical and Emotional Changes | Healthdirect. https://www.healthdirect.gov.au/puberty-for-girls

Healthy habits: menstrual hygiene. (2024, May 7). Water, Sanitation, and Environmentally Related Hygiene (WASH). https://www.cdc.gov/hygiene/about/menstrual-hygiene.html

How oversharing on social media could put your personal information at risk | Information Technology Services. (n.d.). https://its.uky.edu/news/how-oversharing-on-social-media-could-put-your-personal-information-risk

How to Explain Menstruation to Your Daughter - Dillets. https://www.dillets.com/how-to-explain-menstruation-to-your-daughter/

Resources & References

Hygiene: pre-teens and teenagers. (2024, May 22). Raising Children Network. https://raisingchildren.net.au/pre-teens/healthy-lifestyle/hygiene-dental-care/hygiene-pre-teens-teens

Insightful_Ink. (2023, August 19). Embracing Body positivity: Celebrating diversity for a healthier society. *Mindless Mag.* https://www.mindlessmag.com/post/embracing-body-positivity-celebrating-diversity-for-a-healthier-society

Jd. (2020, December 21). *How Brian Tracy sets goals.* Getting Results. https://gettingresults.com/how-brian-tracy-sets-goals/

Kenny, S. (2020, December 16). *I'm a life coach for teens — this is my advice for handling 'Mean girls.'* Scary Mommy. https://www.scarymommy.com/life-coach-teens-advice-handling-mean-girls

Lmft, E. M. (2024, March 1). How to stop comparing yourself to others: This might be why you feel like you're never good enough. - therapy in a nutshell. *Therapy in a Nutshell.* https://therapyinanutshell.com/how-to-stop-comparing-yourself-to-others/

Maves, M., MD. (n.d.). *Smells like teens and tweens: How to deal with body odor.* https://childrenswi.org/newshub/stories/teen-body-odor

Mckenzie, E., & Mckenzie, E. (2024, July 26). Acceptance of body diversity: celebrating every shape and size in the fashion world. *East Hills Casuals.* https://www.easthillscasuals.com/blogs/news/acceptance-of-body-diversity-celebrating-every-shape-and-size-in-the-fashion-world?srsltid=AfmBOoqvDvTilDzru1RmrhuPYnPZdiAlKB3kOKiTHcl-Qx6ABInRtLvH

MyTutor. (2023, May 18). *The psychology of goal setting for teens | MyTutor.* https://www.mytutor.co.uk/blog/parents/educational-advice/goal-setting-for-teens/

National Library of Medicine. (n.d.). *Puberty.* https://medlineplus.gov/puberty.html

Louwagie, L. (2023, July 9). *Home - New Moon Girls*. New Moon Girls. https://newmoongirls.com/

Ortega, S., Ortega, S., & Ortega, S. (2022, August 17). *Gaining self-love for teen girls for overall good mental health*. Step up for Mental Health - to Educate. Fight Causes. Change Minds on Mental Health. https://www.stepupformentalhealth.org/gaining-self-love-for-teen-girls-for-overall-good-mental-health/

Parenting, N. (2023, February 6). *Educating teens to make good choices about themselves and their future*. Nurturing Parenting. https://www.nurturingparenting.com/blog/educating-teens-to-make-good-choices-about-themselves-and-their-future/

Physical development in girls: What to expect during puberty. (n.d.). HealthyChildren.org. https://www.healthychildren.org/English/ages-stages/gradeschool/puberty/Pages/Physical-Development-Girls-What-to-Expect.aspx

Premenstrual syndrome (PMS) - Symptoms & causes - Mayo Clinic. (2022, February 25). Mayo Clinic. https://www.mayoclinic.org/diseases-conditions/premenstrual-syndrome/symptoms-causes/syc-20376780

Puberty: normal growth and development in girls. (n.d.). Saint Luke's Health System. https://www.saintlukeskc.org/health-library/puberty-normal-growth-and-development-girls

Public Opinion. (2016, December 30). 4-H: Important decisions for teens. *Chambersburg Public Opinion*. https://www.publicopiniononline.com/story/life/2016/12/30/4-h-important-decisions-teens/95753200/

Randi. (2020, December 11). *Why Comparing Ourselves to Others is Dangerous and How to Stop It*. Randi Latzman. https://survivingmomblog.com/trauma-and-hardships/why-comparing-ourselves-to-others-is-dangerous-and-how-to-stop-it/

Rosas, K. (2023, June 19). *Menstrual cup folds + tips for getting your cup to open*. Period Nirvana. https://www.periodnirvana.com/menstrual-cup-folds/

Sleep in adolescents. (n.d.). https://www.nationwidechildrens.org/specialties/sleep-disorder-center/sleep-in-adolescents

Smith, S. S. (2012). The influence of stress at puberty on mood and learning: Role of the α4βδ GABAA receptor. *Neuroscience, 249*, 192–213. https://doi.org/10.1016/j.neuroscience.2012.09.065

Social Media dos & don'ts | North Myrtle Beach, SC. (n.d.). https://www.nmb.us/299/Social-Media-Dos-Donts#:~:text=Always%20verify%20friend%2Ffollower%20requests,anything%20else%20sent%20to%20you.

Styzek, K. (2023, March 12). *3 ways to handle a mean girl - WikiHow*. wikiHow. https://www.wikihow.com/Handle-a-Mean-Girl

The benefits of movement and exercise for teenage girls | Nuffield Health. (n.d.). https://www.nuffieldhealth.com/article/the-benefits-of-movement-and-exercise-for-teenage-girls#:~:text=Encouraging%20your%20daughter%20to%20develop,related%20problems%20as%20an%20adult.

The GMC Group. (2021, August 26). *Teen breathe - breathe*. Breathe. https://www.breathemagazine.com/teen-breathe/

The Royal Women's Hospital. (n.d.-b). *Exercise, diet & periods*. https://www.thewomens.org.au/health-information/periods/healthy-periods#:~:text=A%20healthy%20diet%2C%20avoiding%20salt,reducing%20moodiness%20and%20painful%20periods.

The Ultimate Goal setting Process: 7 Steps to Creating Better goals. (2020, June 15). Lucidchart. https://www.lucidchart.com/blog/7-steps-to-creating-better-goals

Thrive Training and Consulting. (2022, November 28). *How Teens Benefit from Helping Others - Thrive Training Consulting*. Thrive

Training Consulting. https://www.thrivetrainingconsulting.com/how-teens-benefit-from-helping-others/

Top 10 internet safety rules. (2019, June 18). /. https://usa.kaspersky.com/resource-center/preemptive-safety/top-10-internet-safety-rules-and-what-not-to-do-online

Toxic shock syndrome - Symptoms & causes - Mayo Clinic. (2022, March 23). Mayo Clinic. https://www.mayoclinic.org/diseases-conditions/toxic-shock-syndrome/symptoms-causes/syc-20355384

User, S. (n.d.). *Eating well: Important for pubertal girls - Puberty2-Menopause*. https://www.puberty2menopause.com/index.php/women-health-resources/i-am-below-18-years-old/puberty/eating-well-important-for-pubertal-girls

What is a Growth Spurt During Puberty? (2024, June 20). Johns Hopkins Medicine. https://www.hopkinsmedicine.org/health/wellness-and-prevention/what-is-a-growth-spurt-during-puberty#:~:text=Peak%20growth%20for%20girls%20is,two%20years%20later%20than%20girls.

Why body positivity is important. (n.d.). https://www.blueridgetreatment.com/post/why-body-positivity-is-important

Why exercise is wise (for teens). (n.d.). https://kidshealth.org/en/teens/exercise-wise.html

Wong, D. (2023, December 16). *How teens can make good decisions every single time (7 proven steps)*. Daniel Wong. https://www.daniel-wong.com/2023/12/16/how-to-make-the-right-decision/

Writer, P. (2022, March 21). *Teen Body Image - The Dangers of Comparing Yourself to Others - PakMag*. PakMag. https://pakmag.com.au/teen-body-image-the-dangers-of-comparing-yourself-to-others/

Made in the USA
Columbia, SC
21 June 2025

12d0f6d9-d88c-4b3e-b420-ee436a229f23R01